the POWER *of a* MAN

USING *Your* INFLUENCE as a MAN *of* CHARACTER

RICK JOHNSON

Revell

a division of Baker Publishing Group
Grand Rapids, Michigan

Published by Revell
a division of Baker Publishing Group
P.O. Box 6287, Grand Rapids, MI 49516-6287
www.revellbooks.com

Printed in the United States of America

Library of Congress Cataloging-in-Publication Data
Johnson, Rick, 1956–
    The power of a man : using your influence as a man of character / Rick Johnson.
        p.   cm.
    Includes bibliographical references.
    ISBN 978-0-8007-3249-3 (pbk.)
    1. Men (Christian theology) 2. Character. 3. Influence (Psychology)—Religious aspects—Christianity. I. Title.
BT703.5.J64 2009
248.8'42—dc22   2008040546

Published in association with the literary agency of WordServe Literary Group, Ltd., 10152 S. Knoll Circle, Highlands Ranch, CO 80130.

This book is dedicated to all good men past, present, and future. You make a difference.

Contents

Acknowledgments

No book ever gets written and published by one person—the author is just fortunate enough to get the credit for it. With that in mind I'd like to acknowledge and thank the following people:

My agent, Greg Johnson, for his wisdom and guidance.

My most excellent editor, Dr. Vicki Crumpton. We've worked on many books together, and she thinks more like a man than most men do (that's a compliment, Vicki). Even though all my best writing ends up quivering on the cutting room floor, slashed and bleeding from your razor-sharp red pen, your contributions make people think I am a much better writer than I really am.

The great team of people at Revell/Baker Publishing, including Suzie Cross (for putting up with me), Twila Bennett (for believing in my vision when many others didn't), Katy Pent (for her support, encouragement, enthusiasm, and prayers), Claudia Marsh (for promoting my books), Deonne

Beròn (publicity), and Dan Baker (for introducing me to Choice Books).

I would be remiss if I did not acknowledge at least some of the men who taught me what it means to be a man—and most of them wrote about it better than I am able: Dr. Frank Pittman, Stu Weber, Steve Farrar, John Eldredge, Ken Canfield, Patrick Morley, and Michael Gurian.

Finally, I'd like to thank my dad, Richard Landsverk, for being proud of me, and for being a man I can be proud to call my father. Those two things make a big difference in my life.

You have a chance to define a new kind of manhood. If you do it well, it will be a manhood in which men do not cheapen themselves and the women around them by the kind of casual, brittle talk that turns women into objects and sex into sport. It will be a manhood in which men see the effects of their gestures and words and most well-intentioned actions. . . . It will be a world where we can love together, laugh together, and work together without fear and without judgment; a world of celebration, not a world of accusation and apology and unexamined assumptions.

Kent Nerburn, *Letters to My Son*

So many men I talk to say they are living only for duty, be responsible . . . lonely, always "on," no one there for them, no one they can depend on, no meaning to life, the pressure is always on. We buy into our culture's myth of "putting our nose to the grindstone" in order to be successful in life as young men. Then we wake up in our forties, unhappy, realizing we've done nothing of significance with our lives. And we unintentionally pass on that vision of life to our boys as well. So many "normal" adolescent males reach college age with holes inside themselves, deep holes they will fill later, in their twenties, with money, status, or some other real or illusionary power.

Michael Gurian, *A Fine Young Man*

1

Raging Bull

First Words

ONCE UPON A TIME there was a man who had been raised in an alcoholic (drug addicted/dysfunctional/abusive—you fill in the blank) home. It was a fearful environment and he was afraid a lot. He hated those feelings even as a young boy because they made him feel "unmanly."

When he was twelve years old, he found out during a drunken argument between his parents that his father was actually his stepfather. It explained why his "father" had so much contempt for him and wanted nothing to do with him.

About this time the boy made a huge discovery. He realized that if he just got mad, he did not have to feel those humiliating emotions of being scared and afraid any longer. As the boy grew into adolescence, he became very angry. He became known as the "fighting guy," and many other kids were afraid of him. He was angry because he was actually afraid. Everything was so difficult. Without a positive male role model to show him how a man lives life, makes decisions, and solves problems, the young man was forever having to discover things on his own. It was frustrating because he made many mistakes and often had to do things over and over again until he figured them out on his own. Failing at things also caused him to be humiliated and angry. Other kids laughed at him when he messed up. As his anger and frustration mounted, he began to strike out at others. He wanted to hurt them before they could hurt him or, even worse, laugh at him and mock him for his failures. Worst of all, the young man did not know *how* to be a man, or even if he *was* a man. He had never been shown how a successful, authentically masculine man lives and succeeds at life. So he tried all the things that the world told him would make him manly—he bedded fatherless girls, he was prideful, he fought those who he perceived were disrespectful to him, he worked hard, he drank large quantities of booze, he smoked cigarettes, and he became a loner.

Life became about survival, and so even though he was smart and athletic, school, grades, sports, college scholarships, and even the future were of less importance than surviving and protecting his heart.

He grew older and became an island—a rock of ice. And he was alone, never needing anyone, because then he would never have to take a chance on being hurt again by anyone. He took drugs to dull the pain and fill the void he felt. He was a hard man—he didn't cut himself or anyone else any slack.

And he was miserable. But it would not be manly to admit pain, fear, and uncertainty. So he stuffed it deep within himself. Because that's what real men do. Or so he thought.

Because of all these reasons, he made poor choices early in his life. In his rage and anger against the injustice of being a lost and lonely man who did not know how to navigate the difficulties of life, he grasped at other role models of masculinity who seemed "manly" to him. He followed their leadership and lived a self-centered existence, using others for his own personal gratification.

That man was me—before I came to terms with my masculinity and understood the power God had endowed me with as a man.

And so go the lives of thousands, perhaps millions, of men in this country and other countries around the world. Men who are not taught a meaningful lesson of what it means to be a man, who just settle for a life of existence and then oftentimes make the lives of those around them miserable. Men who grow up not knowing if or whether they are finally men and what that role means. Men who yearn for that confirmation but are afraid to ask for fear of the answer they might receive. Men who have been programmed from childhood to make negative choices they seemingly have no control over.

Men who have had no father or a poor role model for a father figure are left to discover the secrets of masculinity on their own. It can be a frightful, frustrating, and depressing challenge without a guide. They yearn for authenticity, but no matter how hard they try, they never quite seem to be able to grasp it, always feeling like it's just outside their reach. Oftentimes men from these kinds of backgrounds end up in any one of several scenarios:

- he is in prison;
- he is forced to marry a girl he didn't love because he impregnated her;
- he is addicted to drugs, alcohol, sex, or work;
- he abandons his family;
- or, at best, he settles for living out a shallow life of redundancy and despair because it was just good enough to be acceptable even though it did nothing to inflame his passions or satisfy his longing for significance.

Even those men who do not start out life with traumatic beginnings often fall short of the glory and significance we all dream about and yearn for in our hearts.

So what is a man? Even of greater interest, what exactly is a *good* man? What character traits, roles, and actions distinguish a man who is a good man from one who isn't so good? To take it one step further, what makes a *great* man?

A Stand-Up Guy

Acknowledge your male characteristics. Celebrate them. Honor them. Turn them into a manhood that serves the world around you. But do not let them overwhelm you and do not let those who confuse maleness and manhood take your manhood from you. Most of all, do not fall prey to the false belief that mastery and domination are synonymous with manliness.

Kent Nerburn, US theologian and author,
Letters to My Son

I once had a friend (who I always thought was a manly kind of guy) tell me I was a "man's man." I felt really proud that he called me that. In fact, I thought it was one of the greatest compliments I'd ever received. Receiving it from a man I looked up to made it that much more satisfying. But later, I realized I wasn't sure exactly what he meant. And I was too embarrassed to go back and ask him. I had an idea about what a real man was, but I didn't have a very clear definition from my childhood or our culture. It was a subject that nagged at my gut. Having been raised without a powerful or even a positive role model of masculinity, I have devoted much study to the subject over the course of my life. I always wanted to be masculine, to be a "man's man," but I never really felt as if I measured up to some obscure and unattainable standard. I wasn't even sure what that standard was. Most guys I know secretly wonder the same thing: What does it mean to be "manly," to be a man? To be a stand-up guy, a man of character?

First things first, what exactly is a "man"? It all depends upon who you ask. Ask a woman and you'll likely get a completely different answer than if you ask a man. Ask a young man and you'll get a version differing from the one you would get if you ask an old man. Ask a lumberjack and a male hair stylist and you'll probably get two vastly different versions as well. And that's just in modern America. What about other countries, cultures, and civilizations throughout history?

Before I became a full-time author and speaker, I owned a company where many of my clients were wealthy real estate developers, attorneys, and bank presidents. Today, I spend a fair amount of my time speaking to men in maximum security prisons. I don't exaggerate when I say that the code of masculinity and what it takes to be a man while incarcerated in prison is drastically different than what constitutes a "man" in the corporate boardroom. In fact, men from either one of those environments probably could not survive in the other.

In the following chapters of this book, we'll look at several models of masculinity and compare them. In order to be a "man," especially a good man, we have to know what a man looks like and how he acts. For those of us who did not have that modeled, it can be a huge challenge trying to figure it out.

Challenges as You Read On

All men struggle with the same issues—we just don't talk about them very often. Kent Nerburn sums it up this way:

> I have felt myself emptied into the mystery of the universe, and I have had moments when the smallest slight threw me into a rage.
>
> I have carried others when I barely had the strength to walk myself, and I have left others standing by the side of the road with their hands outstretched for help.
>
> Sometimes I feel I have done more than anyone can ask; other times I feel I am a charlatan and a failure. I carry within me the spark of greatness and the darkest of heartless crimes.
>
> In short, I am a man, as you are.[1]

As I researched this book, I discovered some things that challenged my concepts and perceptions of the "traditional" roles of masculinity. At fifty-one years old, I thought I had finally gotten a grasp on my own masculinity and what constitutes being a man. But many of the traditional concepts I was raised with do not apply today, if they ever did.

For instance, I have a great friend who is a physician, a medical doctor. On the outside he appears to be a very soft-spoken, gentle man. He is a healer, a nurturer. He is slight of build, polite, and physically unimposing. At first glance he would not strike one as a particularly masculine example of manhood. You would never expect him to be a dynamic leader of his family and the community. Yet he leads his family with passion, conviction, and love. He and his wife have raised a family of gifted, emotionally healthy children who have benefited greatly by his steady guidance and firm resolution. His enthusiasm toward life is contagious. He mentors medical students and works with and supports a variety of nonprofits. He is filled with a steel-hardened character that has allowed him to overcome setbacks and disappointments that would have dropped a lesser man to his knees. Yet he faces them with grace, dignity, and a positive attitude of perseverance and faith that inspires me to be a stronger man myself. Were I to have judged him by outward appearances, I would likely have missed the experience of learning a great lesson about masculinity: it is about what's inside a man—not necessarily how he looks or acts, poses and postures, or presents himself—that counts.

Some of this book will be fun to read and some of it will be painful. Hopefully, together we will examine ourselves as men and help each other define what authentic masculinity means to us (at least in this generation) as individuals and as a collective gender. At best, I hope it gives all of us a guide to pass healthy masculinity on to those following in our footsteps and to those who look to us to provide a way to live a life of significance and meaning. Additionally, I hope it makes better the life of any man struggling to understand his own masculinity.

This book is not intended as some brilliant treatise on masculinity authored by a scholarly academic. I read many of those kinds of books in preparation for this book, though. Frankly, it's my opinion that most of those authors know less about authentic masculinity than my auto mechanic does. It strikes me that these authors are more interested in exploring the feminization of males in order to appease their feminist sisters than they are in actually defining manhood. And in their cynicism and sophistication, they make fun of the "archaic" manhood principles of honor, courage, and integrity.

This book is more about me, my journey, and the discoveries I've made. If anything, it is a testament to the struggle that most of us men face trying to discover and understand our own masculinity and what it means to be a "man" today. Hopefully my journey, my failures, and my hard-learned lessons will resonate with other men who have felt the same way I did most of my life: confused, angry, and anxious. Because we all face the same struggles, perhaps together we can define a vision of healthy masculinity that will bless those under our leadership.

This is a book for men on what authentic masculinity is all about. What does a man of character and integrity look like? How does he act and how does he live his life? What is his impact on his family and the world? How does one become authentically masculine? Who are some examples of men of character? How has masculinity been described throughout history, and how has it changed in today's modern world? Those who read this book will understand what healthy masculinity means in a defiant and dangerous world that is afraid of real men.

My goal is that this be an honest book, one that's open and shoots from the hip. Men, young and old, need straight answers to hard questions about what a man is and how he acts. I can remember as a young man being confused about whether or not I was a man, faking it when I was younger, and now finally feeling confident and comfortable—believing I am a man, and feeling good about it—really good. Once I learned a few key factors that made everything fall into place, I quickly emerged into a more healthy, authentic masculinity. It's a man's job to pass those things on to the younger generation following in his footsteps.

Our sons need to know what it means to be a man, a husband, a father—they need to know how a man loves a woman. Our daughters desperately need to know what to look for in a man so they do not make choices that emotionally, physically, psychologically, intellectually, and economically impoverish them and their children. We men need to understand the gift of influence that God has given us so that we treat it responsibly and break the generational sins, curses, and cycles that devastate the lineage of many men's families. After all, a man armed only with a fork in a land of soup does not fare very well.

Will some people criticize or even be angry about what is in this book? Probably—actually, I hope so. But that's okay. As Winston Churchill said, "You have enemies? Good. That means you've stood up for something, sometime in your life." If this book helps you understand your own manhood better, then just take what's in it and don't worry about what anyone else thinks. Many of those who talk the most about what men should be like or how they should act are the ones who know the least about what it actually means to be a man.

I don't know that I have all the answers. But I do know one thing. This country, this world, *needs* you. We need good men who understand what it really means to *be* a man. So go, and make the world a better place because you were here. Be a man. Be a *good* man. Be a stand-up guy.

2

The Good, the Bad, and the Ugly

Masculine Power

THE VAST MAJORITY of men *want* to be good men. They yearn to be men that others look up to and admire. Even the men I speak to in prisons wanted to be good men—something just went wrong along the way.

Let's look at some examples of masculinity to see where we fit into that spectrum. Without something to measure ourselves against, it is impossible to understand where we want to end up.

The Good

God created men as magnificent creatures in his own image. The creator of the universe made men in *his* image. Think about that for a moment. Being created in that image comes with the capacity to impact the world. As men, we have the potential to change the world so much more than most of us ever realize. Did we men forget we had this ability, or did we never know? In their book, *The Hidden Value of a Man*, Gary Smalley and John Trent say it this way:

> How could men not realize how powerful they are? How could they fail to comprehend their vast and terrible ability to touch the lives of their families for good . . . or for unspeakable harm?[1]

The writer of Psalms says this of man: "You made him a little lower than the heavenly beings and crowned him with glory and honor. You made him ruler over the works of your hands; you put everything under his feet: all flocks and herds, and the beasts of the field, the birds of the air, and the fish of the sea, all that swim the paths of the seas" (Ps. 8:5–8).

That verse says we have been crowned with *glory* and *honor*. How many of us live our lives as if we truly understand that endowment? Men have been given a tremendous power to influence the lives of other people. People we will never meet are being impacted by what we do or don't do right now. Future generations are being directed by our actions or inactions today. Our wives and children are looking to us to provide leadership in their lives that they cannot get anywhere else but from us. We have more influence in the lives of our families than any other person walking the face of this earth. Do we take that responsibility seriously? Many men do, and the lives of people around them are blessed mightily. But those who do not recognize the power they hold in their hands waste that gift and let those under their influence shrivel and die.

The Psalms quotation above also says we are rulers over all of God's creation—we have been given authority on earth. A ruler has tremendous power. We need to understand that gift and become good stewards of it. With enormous power comes huge responsibility.

Men who wisely use this influence can lift up the lives of those in their sphere of influence higher than they could ever be without such men in their lives. When men are involved in the lives of women and children, they bless their lives and make them fruitful.

The senior pastor of my church, Randy, is a good man. Randy was stricken with polio as a child and has what appear to be significant physical challenges, yet they don't seem to limit him in any capacity. In addition, after having raised three beautiful and talented daughters almost to adulthood, he and his wife unexpectedly became pregnant with twins. One of the twins, Samuel, was born with Down syndrome and required several open-heart surgeries to repair a hole in his heart. Today, the twins are eight years old. Samuel can be quite challenging on his best days. But the love and patience Randy shows toward him is inspiring and a glimpse of God's love and patience for us, his handicapped children. In fact, Randy readily admits that Samuel has brought a joy and love into his life that he had never experienced before, despite the formidable challenges he presents on a day-to-day basis. Under another man's guidance and protection, Samuel might never have been born or would at least be leading a very different and possibly difficult existence. But under Randy's, he is blossoming.

Randy is an inspiration and a spiritual mentor to many. His example in facing everyday challenges head-on, beyond his already formidable duties as a pastor, changes the lives of many people. Frankly, I am much more comfortable with a pastor who has been through struggles and had to rely on God, rather than one who is "perfect" and has never faced significant challenges in life. Randy has made a big difference in my life and the lives of his family, congregation, and men under his tutelage.

I have another friend whose wife has a debilitating illness. She requires around-the-clock care and is very difficult to manage. In order to care for her and their children, he has had to sacrifice his career and all his personal hopes and ambitions. As we talked one day, I shared with him how much I admired him and how difficult it must be in his situation. He replied, "It is hard, but I believe that God prepared me to be in this situation. With another man, she might have been abandoned and forced to live on the streets. I believe that I am giving my wife the best life she could ever have."

Wow, that is a good man!

Good men lay their lives down for others, sometimes sacrificing their own ambitions for the benefit of those under their care. They put their interests behind the benefit of others. Good men defend the weak and give honor to those around them. A good man is the grandfather who, having already raised a family of his own, willingly raises a grandchild who needs him. A good man works hard day after day to provide for his family even when he hates what he does for a living. A good man stays with and cares for his wife even though she has an illness that devastates the family. This kind of sacrificial love "lays down his life for another," usually not even getting any credit for it. A good man serves others by using his power to lift them up to be more than they could

24

ever be if he were not involved in their lives. He makes their lives better for having been there.

Know this, men—you matter! Your life is important! You are significant and valuable! Don't ever let anyone tell you any different.

The Bad

> As boys without bonds to their fathers grow older and more desperate about their masculinity, they are in danger of forming gangs in which they strut their masculinity for one another, often overdo it, and sometimes turn to displays of fierce, macho bravado and even violence.
>
> Frank Pittman, *Man Enough*

You don't have to be a cruel dictator who murders his people by the thousands like Idi Amin or Saddam Hussein or even a serial killer like Jeffrey Dahmer to be a bad man. You can be an average guy who neglects his responsibilities and uses his power and creativity for his own self-gratification. You can be the guy who charges out of the stands at a Little League game to scream at and demean his son in front of everyone. You can be the guy who sexually molests his step-daughter—just once. You can be the guy who gambles the mortgage on a horse race or spends the kids' food money on drugs. Or the guy who abandons his wife and children when they become a nuisance or difficult. Or if you are truly messed up, you could be one of the members of a gang that gang-rape a pre-teen girl to "initiate" her into the family.

In fact, our culture glorifies unhealthy masculinity. Take someone like Joe Francis, the creator of the *Girls Gone Wild* videos. He spends his time and energy (the power and influence God has given him as a man) taking advantage of and exploiting young women by convincing drunken college girls to take their clothes off and act in sexually provocative ways on camera, in order to make money off of their misguided attempts to be loved and accepted.

Then Francis (and others like him) gets prime-time interviews and is on the news of all the major networks, which only serves to promote his activities and glorify his persona, rewarding him monetarily for his selfishness. And so boys and young men see this example of masculinity as worthy of emulating because of the positive feedback a man like this receives from our culture. (It also perpetuates the stereotype of women as sexual objects to young men.)

Bad men use others in life for their own self-gratification. They contribute nothing positive to anyone's life but their own. Bad men are confused about their masculinity.

But at least a bad man isn't ugly—yet.

The Ugly

In the movie *The General's Daughter*, a young woman is a cadet at West Point. She is the top of her class, putting the male cadets to shame by soundly trouncing them both intellectually and during physical training exercises. In her sophomore year during a large-scale night training operation, she is separated from her unit. Six men from another unit, who hate her for besting them, beat her, stake her to the ground, and brutally gang-rape her the entire night, nearly killing her. At dawn she is finally found by her unit and rushed to the hospital. Her father, a general in the Army, is notified and rushes to the hospital. But along the way he stops first for a meeting with a higher ranking general and is convinced that it would be in the best interest of the Army, the country, the Academy, and his career if this whole "episode" were forgotten. At the hospital his daughter is joyful to see her powerful father with the ability and connections to avenge this terrible crime against her. Surely he will be her hero and make sure justice is served. But to her disbelief and tragic sorrow, he tells her to just forget it ever happened. He crushes his daughter's soul by betraying her love and trust when she needs him most of all, for the sake of his career and a misguided sense of patriotism.

After watching this movie, I thought to myself, *An uglier man never walked the face of the earth—one who would abuse his daughter's trust and love for his own benefit*, until I read about the terrorists in Iraq who strapped bombs on two mentally challenged women and detonated them by remote control in Baghdad markets.

I believe that men, specifically good men, are the key to curing every problem society struggles with. Of course men also cause many of the problems in the world. If we do not understand how to raise boys to become healthy men, we will never be able to solve the problems our society faces. Uncontrolled or unhealthy masculinity can do great damage. We see it in families across our country that have been abandoned, or worse, abused by the men in their homes. One only need look at the statistics and examples of what happens when good men are *not* involved to see the devastation it causes.

All men are capable of ugly behavior given the right circumstances and situation. The Stanford Prison Experiment was a psychological study of human responses to captivity and its behavioral effects on both authorities and inmates in prison. It was conducted in 1971 by a team of researchers led by Philip Zimbardo of Stanford University. Undergraduate volunteers played the roles of both guards and prisoners living in a mock prison in the basement of the Stanford psychology building.

Prisoners and guards rapidly adapted to their roles, stepping beyond the boundaries of what had been predicted, leading to dangerous and psychologically damaging situations. One-third of the guards were judged to have exhibited "genuine" sadistic tendencies, while many prisoners were emotionally traumatized and two had to be removed from the experiment early.

The experiment quickly grew out of hand. Prisoners suffered—and accepted—sadistic and humiliating treatment from the guards. The high level of stress progressively led them from rebellion to inhibition. By experiment's end, many showed severe emotional disturbances.[2]

There are many other experiments and situations, including the Abu Ghraib military prisoner torture and abuse scandal and even Jane Elliott's famous Blue Eyes/Brown Eyes experiment, that appear to show that the darker side of humankind's nature can be readily accessed given the right circumstances.

In other countries around the world, such as Dafur, Sudan, Bosnia, Afganistan, and Rwanda to name a few, men are at the root cause of horrible atrocities—mass rape, murder, genocide, crimes against humanity, and war crimes perpetrated upon hundreds of thousands of innocent women and children. Even national tragedies such as Hurricane Katrina bring out the best and the worst in men. The destruction of New Orleans opened the doors for multitudes of men to prey upon innocent people by looting, pillaging, rape, robbery, murder, and destruction of property. Yet others, like the US Coast Guard, worked heroically and ceaselessly to save the lives of thousands of stranded and devastated victims.

But those are images of manhood that we do not have to confront and face directly. What does ugly masculinity look like up close and personal? Sometimes monsters lurk in the shadows of your own street.

Westley Allan Dodd grew up a few years behind me in my hometown of Richland, Washington. He grew up in what has been described as a loveless home and was often neglected by his parents in favor of his two younger brothers. His parents divorced when he was thirteen. He was also ostracized in school and was reportedly deprived of or denied any emotional growth.

Dodd was conscious of his sexual attraction to neighborhood boys by age nine. He began sexually abusing children when he was thirteen years old; his first victims were his own cousins. All of his victims (over 50 of them) were children below the age of ten. Dodd became more deranged the older he became (he wrote about wanting to castrate his victims and eat their genitals). When he was arrested, the police found with him a homemade torture rack. Here are some of the lowlights of Dodd's sick life on earth.

- Dodd's friend described to him about how his stepdad had to use a catheter to urinate. Later, Dodd would begin experimenting with his body and would insert straight pins and the filler of ink pens like a catheter. Dodd said that he would trick his victims by saying that he could do tricks "kind of like a sword swallower" to lure them to his house, and then he would molest them.

- He molested his own eight-year-old cousin in a closet and her six-year-old brother later that day.

- He was asked to fill in for a neighbor's usual babysitter and molested their two sons, ages one and four, and their three-year-old daughter as they slept.

- Several of the victims he molested included the three-year-old daughter of his dad's girlfriend, his own ten-year-old stepbrother, and his neighbor's two- and four-year-old boys on countless occasions.

- He began choosing the most vulnerable children, including a roommate's two-year-old son, who was partially deaf and could not talk. When the boy resisted, Dodd tied his hands with a bathrobe strap.

Dodd soon began to fantasize about killing his victims, stating, "The more I thought about it, the more exciting the idea of murder sounded. I planned many ways to kill a boy. Then I started thinking of torture, castration, and even cannibalism."

Dodd chose the first child he would murder. His first victim was to be an eight-year-old boy he met while working as a security guard for a construction site. When Dodd tried to trick the child to go home with him, the child stated that he was going to go get some of his toys, and he ended up telling his mom about Dodd. She called the police. Dodd was arrested, but his sentence was reduced to a "gross misdemeanor" and he spent 118 days in jail, with one year probation.

By 1986, Dodd was back in the Vancouver area, pursuing his interest in children full-time. On June 13, 1987, he was arrested after trying to lure a young boy into a vacant building. Convicted on a misdemeanor count of attempted unlawful imprisonment, he was released in October with yet another order for psychiatric treatment. Dodd went through the motions until his probation expired in the fall of 1988, at which time he promptly abandoned his therapy and went back on the hunt. By that time, he had started to collect his morbid daydreams in a diary, complete with discussion of planned rapes and murders, sketches of a torture rack he planned to build, and details of a private pact with Satan to assist him in obtaining victims. Dodd would later tell authorities he wasn't serious about his bargain with the devil, but his writings suggest otherwise.

On Labor Day 1989, armed with a six-inch fish fillet knife bandaged to his ankle and shoestrings to tie up his victims, he went prowling in Vancouver's David Douglas Park. The night before that hunting trip, he wrote: *If I can get it [the child] home, I'll have more time for various types of rape, rather than just one quickie before murder.* He set his sights on brothers Cole and William Neer, ages eleven and ten. Taking the two of them home was clearly out of the question, but Dodd bullied them into following him off the beaten track, deeper into some woods, where both boys were bound with shoelaces, sexually abused, and then stabbed to death. Escaping in the nick of time, Dodd fled the scene less than fifteen minutes before a teenage hiker found the mutilated bodies and ran off to call police.

Dodd spent the next few weeks watching the manhunt for him from a distance, filling a scrapbook with press clippings, killing time with masturbation and writing in his diary until the blood lust drove him out to hunt again. On October 29, he drove across the river into Portland, Oregon, and there abducted four-year-old Lee Isely from the playground of an elementary school. Back at Dodd's apartment, the child was molested and photographed in the nude, his ordeal interrupted briefly by a trip to McDonald's and K-Mart, where Dodd shelled out the money for a toy. The sexual abuse resumed once they were back at Dodd's flat, and climaxed at 5:30 the next morning, when Dodd choked his young victim unconscious and finished the job with a rope, suspending Lee's tiny, broken body from a rod in the closet. After work that night, he dumped the body near Vancouver Lake, at the Washington State Game Preserve, where a hunter discovered it the next morning. Dodd burned all the little boy's clothing except his pair of Ghostbusters underwear, which he kept for a trophy.

Dodd's behavior was escalating. His journal stated, *Incident 3 will die maybe this way: He'll be tied down as Lee was in Incident 2. Instead of placing a bag over his head as I had previously planned, I'll tape his mouth shut with duct tape. Then, when ready, I'll use a clothespin or something to plug his nose. That way I can sit back, take pictures and watch him die instead of concentrating on my hands or the rope tight around his neck — that would also eliminate the rope burns on the neck . . . I can clearly see his face and eyes now.*

On November 11, he tried to abduct a young boy from a Vancouver theater, giving up when the child resisted his advances. Two days later, after scribbling another plea to Satan for assistance, he drove to Camas, Washington, to try his luck at another theater. He got the screaming child outside this time, but bolted for his car when witnesses interceded.

Less than two blocks from the theater, his car broke down, and Dodd was captured by the boyfriend of his latest victim's mother and held until police arrived and took him into custody. Dodd soon pleaded guilty to all charges in January 1990, clearing the way for a death sentence six months later. To his dubious credit, Dodd refused to appeal his case or the capital sentence, stating, "I must be executed before I have an opportunity to escape or kill someone within the prison. If I do escape, I promise you I will kill and rape and enjoy every minute of it." He also chose hanging over lethal injection as the method of his execution "because that's the way Lee Isely died."

Dodd mounted the gallows and was hanged by the neck at Walla Walla state prison shortly after midnight on January 5, 1993. He was the first American inmate hanged in nearly three decades.[3]

I can remember shedding tears as I read the horrible, detailed accounts in the newspaper of what had happened to those poor little boys when the story finally came to light. Dodd's behavior truly was as ugly as a man can get.

But was Dodd the epitome of evil incarnate or just a victim himself? If men of character had taken an interest in him and intervened in his life at an early age, would it have saved the lives of those little boys and the other dozens of children he abused? Maybe not, but it seems as though he fell through the cracks enough that he eventually turned from good to bad and finally to ugly.

Whether ugly masculine behavior is caused by environment (parents and peers), nature (born that way), or evil (spiritual) factors, or a combination of all three, doesn't really matter in the end—especially to its victims.

Good masculine behavior leaves a positive legacy to those who it comes in contact with. Bad masculine behavior also creates a legacy, but one that is destructive in nature. The amount of devastation and destruction that ugly masculinity leaves in its wake is like the entrails and gore splattered on the floor of a slaughterhouse. Just like the proverbial bad apple in a barrel, ugly masculinity destroys far beyond proportion to the size of its power and boundaries. It is a cancer that spreads and eats the life out of its victims.

It is the duty of good men to battle ugly masculinity with all the power that God has endowed them with. Without their intervention, humanity, freedom, and civilization is at risk and perhaps eventually doomed to destruction. The world needs heroes—the world needs good men—now more than ever.

3

Gladiator

Defining Masculinity

Masculinity is not something given to you, but something you
gain. And you gain it by winning small battles with honor.

Norman Mailer, *Cannibals and Christians*

BEFORE WE CAN be good men instead of bad or ugly
men, we must have an understanding of what healthy
masculinity looks like. If men are supposed to be masculine,
then what exactly does masculinity mean? What does it mean
to actually *be* a man? We tell boys and young men to act like
a man, be a man, take it like a man; and yet we are not told
why we need to "take it like a man" or "act like a man," much
less *how* to be a man. Without someone to show us how a
man faces life and solves problems, or to at least provide a

valid definition of manliness, we are left to figure out these and other mysteries of life on our own.

Some of the old models of masculinity we've had in the past don't seem to be quite as applicable today. For instance, the "big boys don't cry" mentality isn't accurate anymore, if it ever was. As a man, I have all the same emotions as every other human being. I might not be as in touch with them or even be able to identify them as readily as my wife, but I have feelings nonetheless. Just because I don't make a big deal out of them doesn't mean they don't exist. In addition, society has a very skewed perspective on what it means to be a man—mostly dependent upon wealth, power, toughness, sexual conquests, and the accumulation of material goods.

On the other end of the spectrum, the current cultural push to "feminize" males isn't very comfortable either. It's why so many boys and young men are confused today. We were created different from females for a reason. Frankly, I like those differences—I don't want to be more like a woman. And most women I know *want* men to be men. The positive qualities that both males and females bring to the table, while different, are unique and each equally valuable.

Now some people are looking to define men that exhibit a type of masculinity that combines the best of traditional manliness (strength, honor, character) with positive traits traditionally associated with females (nurturance, communicativeness, cooperation)—sort of an *übersexual* man.

With all those things in mind, let's try to develop an acceptable working definition of maleness, masculinity, and manhood that most of us can be comfortable with. After all, it's pretty difficult to be an authentically masculine man if you don't know what one is.

Past Perspectives

To get an accurate perspective of masculinity, it might be helpful to look at where it has been and where it comes from. Has masculinity evolved or devolved over the history of civilization? Certainly it is different now than it was a thousand years ago.

For a large portion of human history, a man's only role with regard to his family was to hunt for food and provide physical protection. Because those traits have been bred into a man, they are roles men are still most comfortable with even today. But men of previous times may have had a few qualities that separated the men of yesteryear from the "boys" of today.

Down through history, men who were authentically masculine (in addition to whatever other roles they may have had) had "sand"—they would not desert you no matter how tough things got; they would stay and fight. They were tough, rugged, and focused. Men went where no one else dreamed of going—where nothing was safe. They went where life tested them and where the challenges just to survive were insurmountable. They dog sledded to the North Pole and Antarctic, climbed Mount Everest, explored unknown lands teeming with dangerous wild animals, sailed across uncharted oceans on little wooden boats to unexplored lands, mapped the Congo River and the Amazon jungle, and ventured into wilderness areas where no man had ever walked before. Men had to be hard, aggressive, decisive, and reckless in order to survive. It was a kill-or-be-killed world, and you either conquered your circumstances or forfeited your life.

Men have also solved some of the greatest challenges and overcome the biggest obstacles facing humankind. They built the pyramids and other wonders of the world, settled the wild places of earth, and walked on the moon. The majority of the greatest inventions throughout history were made by men—the printing press, the refrigerator, the computer, modern plumbing, the airplane, and hot dogs.

Men developed a way to keep track of time, tame electricity, and cure diseases. They created art, music, medicine, mathematics, science, astronomy, architecture, and written language.

Perhaps the biggest problem men face today is that there is nowhere else to explore. The world is a smaller, safer place to live. There's no danger, at least in the United States, except for what we create for ourselves. There's no challenge except those obstacles we intentionally place in our own path—or have been placed there by others. Some of the biggest challenges we face today are satisfying our wives, raising our children, and trying not to die from boredom before we retire. I exaggerate a bit, but most men know what I'm talking about. The mundane life of getting up, going to work, coming home, eating dinner, playing with the kids for a few minutes, hopefully having sex with your wife occasionally, going to sleep, and getting up and doing it all over again is a confining, if not boring, existence for most men. There's got to be more to life, more to being a man, than this "quiet desperation" that Thoreau refers to.

Is it possible that some men even unconsciously engage in destructive or dangerous activities like addictions or affairs as a way to put some challenge and danger in their lives to fulfill that need?

Unfortunately, today we are not taught to look for challenges to tackle that could be just as heroic, adventurous, and dangerous as yesteryear—things like poverty, abuse, fatherlessness, and abandoned children. There are huge challenges out there that probably only a bunch of strong men together can overcome. For instance, between 100,000 to 300,000 girls are kidnapped and sold into the sex industry here in America. Most of these are "throwaway" kids from foster homes or drug families. Many have been sexually abused from a young age. But some are daughters just like yours and mine who were in the wrong place at the wrong time. The average age of these girls is fourteen to fifteen years old. They are generally transported across several states and sold multiple times. Once captured and traumatized, it is nearly impossible for them to escape on their own. Imagine what it feels like to be in this horrific situation, to believe your captors care nothing about you, using you as a commodity. These girls are exposed only to bad and ugly masculinity. They need good masculinity to come to their rescue.

C'mon, guys, we cannot stand by and let this kind of thing happen to the girls and women under our protection. Not on our watch!

Cultural Expectations

Truthfully, I'm not sure what our current culture expects from men. I don't even think the culture really knows what it expects from men. Therein lies the problem. I do know that men are easy targets—we don't defend ourselves very well against criticism. Hence, most of the problems of our culture tend to be blamed on men, perhaps rightfully so. That power we have been given, when used improperly or ignored, can certainly be destructive.

But masculinity, in and of itself, is not the problem. The problem is the lack of a definition of masculinity, a role model of masculinity, consistent training in a healthy model, and general lack of respect for masculinity. Masculinity is not celebrated or even respected in our culture anymore. More often it is a problem or curse to overcome. Some segments of our culture even refer to males as having "testosterone poisoning." That's a terrible birthright to pin on boys and young men.

Our society typically ascribes a dismal role to men, with low or no expectations of nobility or greatness. Few portrayals of men in the media are positive. Television shows and commercials often cast men as bumbling idiots with their wives as the competent ones in the family—all done under the guise of humor, which makes it acceptable. I wonder what the outcry would be like, though, if they reversed roles and all television sitcoms portrayed women as bumbling idiots and all men as the competent ones.

Before my quest to discover and understand my own manhood, I remember the frustration of trying to understand what society expected of me as a man. I knew I was getting mixed messages and even felt a little alienated. For all the talk of a male-dominated society, I find it interesting that the only class of people who are fair game for discrimination today are males—most specifically Christian males.

I spoke at a church on the topic of "Why Men Matter." This was an inspirational talk on the value of men in families and our society. Afterward, an elderly man approached me and said, "For my whole life as an adult man, over fifty years, all I've ever heard was the faults of masculinity. I've never been told I was important and valuable. To think I wasted all these years feeling bad about myself—thank you so much for telling me I mattered!"

Our culture patterns a somewhat perverted stereotype of what a man should be. Young men raised without fathers are especially confused by the images projected to them by today's professional athletes, rap stars, and movie actors (many who were also raised without positive male role models) who model men as being self-indulgent, self-focused, hedonistic, or even violent.

Hollywood's version of a man's man is a kind of "leader of the pack" alpha male—the kind of man other men look up to and try to emulate. He is typically a womanizer or at least able to charm all women into bed at will. He's rugged, handsome, and tough. He can win against all odds, and he doesn't need any help from man or even God.

We learn early in life that to be successful we have to perform well. Cultural masculinity appears to hinge on the combination of the ability to make money (lots of it), have power, command the adoration of many females, and possess sexual prowess. Here's why these "performance" myths are false and even dangerous.

First of all, hear this clearly. If you have never been told this before, remember this: *money and power mean nothing.* You already have unprecedented power just by virtue of your gender. God has given each man the ability to change the world by himself! How you choose to use that power is another issue.

Money is just a tool. I told my kids as they were growing up that making money is not hard. Anyone can make a lot of money. I've made a lot of money and lost a lot of money in my lifetime. Having owned several businesses, I understand that making money is not difficult if your objective is just to become wealthy. For instance, anyone could start a pornographic website and make tons of money. You can cheat on business deals and take advantage of employees as a business owner and make lots of cash. Some of the most miserable men I know have a lot of money. However, making money with integrity is more difficult; becoming successful while maintaining your moral compass is more of a challenge and requires effort.

Having sex with scores of women is not difficult either. Many women, especially those reared without a father or those who have been abused by men early in life, are easy targets for men without scruples. These women desire masculine affection and validation so much that they willingly (if unwittingly) confuse sex for intimacy. Using women to confirm our manhood is a particularly noneffective tactic many men fall into. In the same way that a mother cannot bestow masculinity upon her son, a woman cannot bestow masculinity upon a man by sleeping with him. We know this in our hearts. Femininity can never bestow masculinity upon us; only masculinity can bestow masculinity. In other words, even though we often consider sexual conquests or even the first act of sexual intercourse as the mark of manhood, a woman (even through sexual union) cannot grant that mantle upon a male. Some of the most immature, childish, and unhappy men I know sleep with a multitude of women.

Television and magazines often project an image of real men as being attracted to "male" behaviors involving fast cars, beer, loose women, and guns. Many of these stereotypes are unhealthy for men and encourage risk-taking behaviors, which can be attractive to men who are bored or unfocused in life. For instance, men drink more alcohol and are more apt to drink and drive, not wear seat belts, and engage in unprotected sexual activities than women. The media encourages those types of attitudes and behaviors in order to sell products.

While some men go on a journey to discover what it means to be a man, some of us are oblivious—not knowing what we don't know. And some (who were fortunate enough to have had a succession of great male role models throughout their lives) just instinctively know what it means to be a man and don't worry all that much about it.

Too often, though, we men settle for judging ourselves by assessing our sexual accomplishments, acquiring material possessions, or conquering other tangible challenges in order to prove our manhood. Generally we do this when we have not had authentic role models to show us how a man acts. We then turn to posturing to try to show the world that we are in fact "men."

We have to find a way to give boys and young men a vision of masculinity that is greater and more inspiring than just making a lot of money or sleeping with as many women as possible.

Manly Definitions

Let's look at the literal definitions of what it means to be a man to get some background. Whereas *maleness* is a biological and physiological classification concerned with the reproductive system, *masculinity* principally refers to socially acquired traits and secondary sex characteristics. *Manhood* is something we attain by combining the elements of the first two roles with acts and deeds. In other words, we are born male and we acquire traits that are deemed masculine, but we must achieve manhood. Masculinity frequently refers to qualities and behaviors judged by a particular culture to be associated with or especially appropriate to men and boys. Direct competition of physical skill and/or strength is a feature of masculinity that appears in some form in virtually every culture on earth. But there are many other factors that separate being masculine from actually being a "man."

Even though masculinity may look different in different cultures, there are common aspects to it that cross cultures. *Machismo* is a form of masculine culture. It includes assertiveness or standing up for one's rights, responsibility or selflessness, a general code of ethics, and respect.

In some cultures, masculinity may be an indicator of social status as much as wealth, race, or social class. In Western culture, for example, greater masculinity usually brings greater social status for males among their peers (a man's man, for example). Many English words such as *virtue* and *virile* (all from the Latin *vir* meaning "man") reflect this. An association with physical and/or moral strength is implied. Masculinity is associated more commonly with men than with boys.[1]

Most of the men I have talked with about the subject of masculinity over the years seem to have a pretty vague or superficial concept of what it means to be a man. They often mention things like strength, provider, protector, and integrity. But I don't think they have a deeper understanding of manhood. They often know what it's *not*, but they are never really sure what it *is*. In other words, they know it when they see it but they can't tell you what it is.

Different men embody different types of masculinity. John Wayne represents one type, whereas Albert Einstein might represent another type—both great men, but polar opposites on the scale of masculinity.

Different countries may have conflicting ideas on what constitutes masculine behavior. While acceptable in the US, in many countries and cultures around the world it is considered unmanly for men to wear short pants. In fact, different areas of the same country may have differing ideas on what constitutes manly behavior. For instance, here in the Pacific Northwest (Portland and Seattle) it is considered somewhat effeminate behavior for a man to use an umbrella, but very acceptable in areas of the country like the East Coast. Men who live in San Francisco probably behave differently on an everyday basis than do men in Laramie, Wyoming.

Influences on Modern Masculinity

Courage is grace under pressure.

Ernest Hemingway

No examination of masculinity would be complete without a discussion about the influence of the writer Ernest Hemingway. Hemingway defined several generations of masculinity for men, at least in Westernized countries. Hemingway's books and short stories were hugely popular from the late 1920s through the 1960s and even today are considered classic American literature. His masculine writing style and powerful prose identified certain male characteristics that have been absorbed into our culture and emulated by men ever since. Hemingway soon became synonymous with manliness in literature.

Most of Hemingway's male characters are portrayed by the tough, macho guy who chooses to live his life by following a "code of honor, courage, chivalry, honesty, and the ability to bear pain with resistance and dignity, and does not whine when defeated."[2] His heroes are typically stoic males who exhibit an ideal described as "grace under pressure." This hero is Hemingway's ideal man, the kind every man should want to become. His characters pursued "manly" endeavors such as boxing, bull fighting, big game hunting, and "winning" women. This code was adopted by Western culture as the pinnacle of masculinity.

Robert Penn Warren writes of the "code" hero:

> [Hemingway's] heroes are not squealers, welchers, compromisers, or cowards, and when they confront defeat they realize that the stance they take, the stoic endurance, the stiff upper lip means a kind of victory. If they are to be defeated they are defeated upon their own terms; some of them have even courted their defeat; and certainly they have maintained, even in the practical defeat, an ideal of themselves—some definition of how a man should behave, formulated or unformulated—by which they have lived. They represent some notion of a code, some notion of honor, that makes a man a man, and that distinguishes him from people who merely follow their random impulses and who are, by consequence, "messy."[3]

Regardless of his influence on masculinity, whatever demons possessed his soul caused Hemingway to end his life in a decidedly unmanly way—with the barrel of a shotgun in his mouth. Of interest as it pertains to our discussion, Hemingway's father committed suicide by shooting himself in the head with a pistol, reportedly because he was despondent about his numerous incurable illnesses. While Hemingway despised his father's actions due to his own personal code of conduct, when he found himself in his later years an alcoholic, injured and in pain, depressed and ill, he too chose to end his life just as his father had modeled. The generational legacy continued as his granddaughter, actress Margaux Hemingway, also committed suicide in 1996.

From Hemingway's portrayal of masculinity came the screen persona of John Wayne. The form of masculinity represented by "the Duke" has come under a lot of criticism lately—and maybe rightly so, although I doubt he would have cared, judging from his quote: "I have tried to live my life so that my family would love me and my friends respect me. The others can do whatever the [blank] they please."

Clearly, though, the loner persona embodied by Wayne's characters is unhealthy for men. But even still, I don't know too many men who aren't secretly attracted to his type of character. Classic movies such as *The Magnificent Seven*, *The Wild Bunch*, *The Searchers*, and *Braveheart* speak to a man's deep sense of need for justice, intestinal fortitude, and rugged individualism. Many actors from that era such as Humphrey Bogart, Robert Mitchum, Steve McQueen, and more recently Clint Eastwood, represented that *type* of masculinity.

The "John Wayne" mentality may be unhealthy for men emotionally, but his characters had a code of conduct they lived by that consisted of great moral convictions. Their attitude seemed to sum up the "Code of the West." This code helped contribute to the United States being the greatest country to ever evolve on the face of the earth. Wayne's character believed in sticking up for the underdog, protecting women and children, fighting fair, taking personal responsibility; he believed in courage, justice, loyalty, and dogged determination despite the odds against him. He suffered in silence and never gave up.

Wayne was dying of cancer during the filming of his last movie, *The Shootist*. One scene required him to shoot his attacker as he was running away from him. While he rested in his trailer, the entire scene was shot except Wayne's part. As the director explained the scene to him, the Duke is rumored to have looked him in the eye and said, "I don't shoot men in the back." He then walked back to his trailer while the entire scene was re-shot.

In the 1950s and early 1960s, Frank Sinatra and his Rat Pack epitomized a swinging, hipper version of masculinity to parallel that provided by John Wayne and Ernest Hemingway. It had similarities but was a classier or richer version more suited to the cultural changes taking place. Sinatra was the well-dressed chairman of the board who drank hard, fought hard, and womanized hard. This masculinity lowered the moral standards and obligations of men to mirror the changes in our culture.

The 1960s and early '70s had a plethora of the spy genre movies like the James Bond, Flint, and Tony Rome series that portrayed men as dashing, cool, deadly, sex machines. These role models tended to lower the bar of masculinity even further.

These cultural stereotypes encouraged a one-dimensional picture of masculinity. As we drifted further away from the "John Wayne" version of masculinity, we inadvertently encouraged men to become even more self-focused and self-absorbed. Hemingway's and Wayne's influence gave us one version of manhood, but it was not a flexible version that all men could feel comfortable with. Or perhaps men do not feel they can live up to this model of masculinity anymore. Certainly the pressure on men to "perform" is as strong as it has ever been.

Today, it seems as if the masculine role models the media projects for young men are bereft of any moral values or principles. Picture in your mind for a moment the images and types of masculinity encouraged by our culture today— are they greater or lesser examples of masculinity than in the past? Maybe I'm just getting old, but they don't seem very noble or inspirational to me.

What a Man Is Not

In the book *Season of Life*, author Jeffrey Marx references a *Washington Post* newspaper article about the deaths by heatstroke of numerous college and high school football players. The article quotes a college lineman who "routinely compensated for dramatic loss of fluids by hooking up to an intravenous line after practice." The player was quoted as saying, "It's all about being a man. Being tough."

A high school football coach was then quoted as saying, "You have to be physically tough on them. You have to push them to the brink and either they are going to break or they are going to stand up and be a man. That's how you change these young boys into being men."

Biff, the high school football coach chronicled in Marx's book, is beyond incredulous at those comments. He says,

We ought to get a lifetime contract to play against this guy. . . . We'd beat them every time we'd play, because he has no idea what he's talking about. . . . Fifty boys together, fifty boys that love each other and that are well affirmed and well loved by their coaches, will smack those guys anytime, in *anything*. Being a father. Being a son. Being a football player. Being a doctor. Being an astronaut. Being a human being. Being anything.

That's not how you become a man. Do you understand me? Because that means to be a man, you gotta somehow be some big, strong, physical person. And that's got nothing to do with it. Trust me.[4]

He's right. Being big, and tough, and strong does not make you a man. Sometimes those traits might be *part* of being a man, but just being those alone does not mean you *are* a man. Some of the biggest, toughest guys I've ever met were the poorest excuses for men that I've ever seen. Those kinds of traits are often imposed upon men in the military or during Special Forces training. The drill instructors might say that they are teaching you to be "a man," but what they are really teaching you is how to defend yourself and others, how to survive, how to react without thinking, and how to kill. Those traits might be a duty *imposed* upon a man during his lifetime in order to fulfill a need, but they do not in and of themselves *make* you a man.

What a Man Is

> Seek justice,
>   encourage the oppressed.
> Defend the cause of the fatherless,
>   plead the case of the widow.
>
> Isaiah 1:17

50

I am optimistic that there is a new kind of masculinity taking hold in this country. Men want to lead more rewarding lives and are recognizing that living for others is the path to true satisfaction.

Have you ever noticed that sometimes you are naturally drawn to a certain type of man? People like being around him. You can't quite put your finger on what it is, but you know you like it. When he comes into a room or walks down the street, people automatically notice him—they see something different about him. There's something invigorating and compelling about him. It's exciting and even a little dangerous to be around him. He's calm but confident, relaxed but prepared, kind but authentic, and bold but compassionate.

You've just encountered authentic masculinity. It's rare, but it's out there.

What is a real man? What does he look like? How does he act? What characteristics separate him from an average guy?

Our culture generally tells us that, at best, the role of a man is to put his nose to the grindstone after finishing school and work hard the rest of his life. It tells us the mark of a man is how much money he makes and how many "toys" he acquires. His financial achievement determines how successful he has been in life. The American Dream is the standard by which we judge the success of a man's life.

Our culture also tells us that men really aren't all that important in the lives of women and children except maybe as providers. Society has spent the better part of the past several decades trying to soften or even feminize our young men and boys. Now we are confused and angry when they don't act more like real men.

51

In fact, our culture seems to consider an authentically masculine man to be dangerous. They would like to emasculate and prevent him from exerting his influence in the world. They use fear, shame, and political correctness to keep him silenced on the sidelines of life.

Men now are caught up in the self-centered, mundane pursuits of life. Most are apathetic and living lives filled with passivity—they lack decisiveness and commitment. They fail to see the higher purpose that they were created for. Even the best of them often feel they are doing enough just by being a "good guy," a caring person who does nice things for others occasionally—when it's convenient, that is. Most men in our country are trapped in societal expectations and the search for self-gratification. All men yearn for something meaningful, a cause to fight for—significance in our lives.

What men fail to realize is that freedom lies in following God's plan for their lives.

An authentically masculine man puts aside his needs, desires, wants, and sometimes even his dreams, for the benefit of others. He does this without fanfare and frequently without anyone even noticing. His life is not about *his* individual rights, achievements, or happiness; it's about making life better for others. His sacrifices are part of his character and give his life significance. He meets these sacrifices with the stoic nobility that God granted all men by right of their birth gender.

Too many boys grow up thinking that manhood is finally having the freedom of not having to do things they don't want to anymore, or doing only what they want. I see fatherless boys who grow up thinking that the world is about them and that women will serve and rescue them from every trouble and inconvenience they experience. But the reality is that being a man actually means being *required* to perform many things you don't want to do. It also means not doing many things you'd like to do.

A real man has honor. He stands tall as the fierce winds of adversity blow around him. He cherishes and protects women and children. He knows he has an obligation to mentor those who follow in his footsteps. He recognizes his sphere of influence and uses it for good. He understands that life does have fundamental truths and lives his life according to a firm set of principles. He uses his God-given warrior spirit to fight for justice and equality. He stands for *something*. Too many men today stand for nothing—they are directionless.

Men who exhibit authentic masculinity live lives of significance. They lift up others to help them achieve their potential. They make sacrifices in order to make a difference in the world—for everyone, not just their own families. They have passion and vision and are genuinely interested in giving of themselves for the betterment of others. And they probably don't make a big production out of doing it either. Men like this are other-centered, not self-centered. They are other-focused instead of self-focused.

In the movie *Kingdom of Heaven*, a young widower black-smith first meets his father as he travels to defend Jerusalem during the Crusades. His father introduces himself to his son for the first time and asks forgiveness for never having been a part of his life. With nothing to keep him in his village after the death of his wife and child, the young man follows his father and trains to become a knight. In the short period they are together before his father's death, the young man flourishes under his father's tutelage and follows in his footsteps, becoming a man of honor. Throughout the movie the young knight relies on his father's instruction and example. In one powerful scene near the end of the movie while he is preparing the city of Jerusalem against attack by overwhelming forces, he endows knighthood upon the city's commoners defending the city by quoting the same oath that his father spoke to him:

> Be without fear in the face of your enemies,
> Be brave and upright that God may love thee,
> Speak the truth even if it leads to your death,
> Safeguard the helpless.
> That is your oath![5]

The local high priest admonishes him by saying, "Who do you think you are? Can you alter the world? Does making a man a knight make him a better fighter?"

As the knight looks him in the eye and boldly proclaims, "Yes!" you can see all the men who have been charged with the challenge to greatness swell with pride and determination. They do in fact know that the expectations and exhortations of greatness can make a man more than he would be without the knowledge of God's vision for his and every man's life.[6]

WHAT'S MANLY, WHAT'S NOT (FOR FUN)	
Manly	**Not So Manly**
Pick-up trucks & SUVs	Mini-van & MINI-Cooper
German Shepherds/Labrador retrievers	Any small "yappy" dog, poodles
Football	Bunko
Pomade	Mousse
Corn beef on rye	Cucumber finger sandwiches
Wallet	Purse

I think it is imperative that we look to the Bible for a moment as a source of defining masculine behavior. If you don't consider yourself a spiritual person, just hear me out. Before becoming a Christian, I spent a year studying in an attempt to disprove the validity and authenticity of Christianity. One thing I learned during my yearlong study was that, regardless of my personal belief system, the Bible contained huge amounts of truths for daily living. At the very least I would encourage you to read those words for their wisdom even if you do not believe the spiritual aspects presented. The books of Proverbs and James were especially helpful to me during my research. If you're looking for a Bible, consider using a New International Version (NIV) or a GOD'S WORD version, as they are more understandable to the average guy. Also use a Bible with annotations at the bottom, which explain what certain passages mean in layman's terms.

Manhood, as defined by the Bible, requires men to put the needs and best interests of others before their own. It's about living sacrificially. A man uses his strength and influence to help others and defend those who cannot defend themselves. Read how manly this verse sounds and how it speaks powerfully to a man's heart:

> I rescued the poor who cried for help, and the fatherless who had none to assist him. . . . I made the widow's heart sing . . . I was eyes to the blind and feet to the lame. I was father to the needy; I took up the case of the stranger. I broke the fangs of the wicked and snatched the victims from their teeth.
>
> Job 29:12, 13, 15–17

Hooah! That verse makes me want to be a man—to break some fangs and snatch victims from the grasp of evil!

God gives men a mandate throughout the Bible to protect women and children and be his representatives here on earth. "Religion that God our Father accepts as pure and faultless is this: to look after orphans and widows in their distress" (James 1:27).

We believe that our Better Dads ministry has the anointing of Isaiah 61 over it, but especially the first verse, "The Spirit of the Lord GOD is upon me, because the LORD has anointed me to bring good news to the afflicted; He has sent me to bind up the brokenhearted, to proclaim liberty to captives, and freedom to prisoners" (NASB). We believe that by helping others we are making a difference in the world and thus justify our existence on earth.

Authentic men are passionate, fierce, and noble—they care. In fact, they are dangerous, but it's a good dangerous. You might not see this passion on the exterior, but it's bubbling under pressure just beneath the surface, forcing its way into every area of their lives. They have a spiritual longing for adventure, for a battle to fight that's bigger than themselves, for significance in their lives. Like modern-day gladiators, they stand in the ring facing the challenges of life with courage and passion.

When you see a man with a passion for something bigger and nobler than himself, you are looking authentic masculinity in the eye.

4

Braveheart

Honor Codes

Because there is very little honor left in American life, there is a certain built-in tendency to destroy masculinity in American men.

Norman Mailer, *Cannibals and Christians*

THROUGHOUT HISTORY, MASCULINITY has had close connection with some sort of honor code. Males appear to have valued honor since the beginning of civilization. Some of these honor codes were noble and uplifting, while others were self-serving or even evil. Let's look at a variety of honor codes and understand why they are important and how to live by them.

What Is an Honor Code?

An *honor code* is a set of principles that govern a community or group of people. It is based on a set of rules or ideals that define what constitutes honorable behavior within that group. The use of an honor code depends on the idea that people (at least within that community) can be trusted to act honorably. Oftentimes there are severe punishments for those who violate the honor code of a culture.

Men need to believe in something worth dying for. They need a code to live by that holds them to a higher standard than they are capable of by themselves. Men will gladly sacrifice their lives if they have an honor code to live by, if they have some truths worthy of sacrifice. Unfortunately, our current culture of relativism has left us with no real truths (everything being relative) and thus nothing worth dying for. Nothing is honorable or noble. Cynicism and apathy rule the day. This philosophy says that everybody's separate beliefs are all true for them, and there are no absolute truths. This makes a belief system or worldview such as pedophilia, animal rights, naturalism (environmentalism), or socialism every bit as important and valuable as the Judeo-Christian belief system that made our country the greatest nation in the history of the world. This worldview says that just because I don't agree with your belief doesn't mean you are wrong and that I shouldn't say anything against it. Of course, this is only true if you toe the line of the prevailing cultural attitude in power at the moment. Try saying something against homosexuality, multiculturalism, the theory of evolution, or abortion rights today and see how fast the "tolerant" ones viciously attack you.

But men who allow themselves to be manipulated or coerced into being passive, apathetic, nonparticipants, and noncombatants are lesser men for it. Not only do they suffer the shame of their own cowardice but their wives and children suffer as a consequence.

Honor, Principles, Ideals

Men crave honor. *Honor* is the relationship between one's virtues or values and their status within a society. I believe that honor is as integral a part of a man's soul as love or faith, and is one of the bonds that establish a person's core character.[1]

The concept of honor appears to have declined in importance in the modern secular Western culture. It appears to be more prevalent in "hot-blooded" Mediterranean cultures such as Italian, Persian, or Arab; or in more "gentlemanly" societies like the "Old South." Feudal or other agricultural societies, which focus upon land use and land ownership, may tend to value honor more than do industrial societies. Traces of the importance attached to honor also linger in the military (officers may conduct a court of honor) and in organizations such as Scouting or sports programs. This might explain why those organizations are attractive to males.

Honor in our culture today is not only less important than in previous times, but it is even scorned. Christianity has encouraged men to turn the other cheek while the "enlightened" left encourages them to favor reason over emotion. Hence men have gravitated to apathy and passivity as the easier road to travel. The West first channeled honor into the form of chivalry, then folded it into a code of manly but magnanimous Victorian gentlemanliness—and now, in the twentieth and twenty-first centuries, it has been driven into disrepute.

An honor code is based upon a set of ideals. An ideal is a principle or value that a man actively pursues as a goal. Ideals are particularly important in ethics. The order in which one places them tends to determine the value given them. For instance, someone who claims to have an ideal of honesty but is willing to lie to protect a friend is demonstrating that, not only does he hold friendship as an ideal, but it is more important to him than honesty.

A different form of ideal is a hero, who is held up as a moral example. I believe all men dream of being heroes. A hero usually fulfills the definitions of what is considered good and noble in the originating culture. Typically the willingness to sacrifice the self for the greater good is seen as the most important defining characteristic of a hero.

Principles are fundamental laws, doctrines, or assumptions that a person or culture lives by. They are a set of rules or code of conduct. For example, a person's ethics may be seen as a set of principles that the individual obeys in the form of rules, as guidance or law. These principles thus form the basis for such ethics.

Ethics is the study of values, morals, and morality. It covers the analysis and employment of concepts such as right, wrong, good, evil, and responsibility.

Men often act erratically because they do not have a code of honor. A code of honor is a set of rules that a man lives by. His code may be personal or based on his connection to a group or organization.

Types of Honor Codes

Honor is at the heart of authentic masculinity. Throughout history men of all races and origins have striven to live lives of honor. Even criminal elements have developed codes of honor (honor among thieves, never snitch, and so forth). Only recently has masculine honor been swept away on the tide of moral relativism. But all men need honor to truly fulfill their destiny.

The French call it *noblesse oblige*—the obligation of honorable, generous, and responsible behavior associated with high rank or birth. Honor seems to be one of the key ingredients in fulfilling a man's life, no matter his nationality or race.

Many of the honor codes have common themes. They usually contain elements of duty, courage, integrity, loyalty, and willingness to die for a greater cause. Here are some specific examples of honor codes throughout history.

Bedouin

The Bedouin tribes of the Arabian Desert have an honor code system called *Sharaf*. *Sharaf* can be acquired, augmented, lost, and regained. *Sharaf* involves protection of the virtue of the women of the family, protection of property, maintenance of the honor of the tribe, and protection of the village if the tribe has settled down. The tribe's justice system is also based on this honor code.

Hospitality is a virtue closely linked to *Sharaf*. If required, even an enemy must be given shelter and fed for some days. Poverty does not exempt one from one's duties in this regard. Generosity is a related virtue, and in many Bedouin societies, gifts must be offered and cannot be declined.

Bravery is also closely linked to *Sharaf.* Bravery indicates the willingness to defend one's tribe for the purpose of tribal solidarity and balance. It is closely related to manliness. Bravery usually entails the ability to withstand pain, including male circumcision.

Mafia

The European Mafia (or *La Cosa Nostra*) was originally founded on a sense of loyalty and respect for culture, family, and the Sicilian heritage. The Mafia's purpose was to protect its members' interests and grant them freedom in business in exchange for absolute loyalty and submission to the "family." The Sicilian Mafia was based on the belief that justice, honor, and vengeance are for a man to take care of, not for a government to take care of. The Sicilian Mafia valued the code of *omertà*, the code of honor and silence. They strictly adhered to the rule that theirs was a secret society, open only to those who shared Sicilian blood.

Knighthood

The knights of medieval England lived under the honor code of *chivalry*. Knights were taught to excel in the arms, to show courage, to be gallant and loyal, and to swear off cowardice and baseness. The knight also represented a cultural ideal of Christian manhood whose honor, valor, and virtue were celebrated throughout the Middle Ages.

Chivalry is usually associated with ideals of knightly virtues, honor, and courtly love. Chivalry disposes men to take heroic actions and helps them value beauty, intellect, and morality.

Christianity had a modifying influence on the virtues of chivalry. The church placed requirements on knights to protect and honor the weaker members of society and also to help the church maintain peace.

Knights Templar was one of the most famous of the Christian military orders. The Templars were both monks and soldiers, making them in effect some of the earliest "warrior monks" in the Western world. Templar vows consisted of chastity, poverty, and obedience.

Samurai

Pre-industrial Japan had a warrior class known as samurai. These warriors lived by the honor code of *Bushido* or the Way of the Warrior. Bushido stressed concepts such as loyalty to one's master, self-discipline, and respectful, ethical behavior. The samurai were trustworthy and honest. They lived frugal lives with no interest in riches and material things, but rather they were interested in honor and pride. They were men of true valor. Samurai had no fear of death. They would enter any battle despite the odds. To die in battle would bring honor to one's family and one's lord. After a defeat, some samurai chose to commit ritual suicide (*seppuku*) by cutting their abdomen rather than being captured or dying a dishonorable death.

Code of the West—Cowboys

During the early push to settle the American West, many of the things men value most were precious and rare. Women were scarce and thus were valued and protected. Kindness and civility toward all women was a given in any situation. A man's gun and his horse were also exceptionally valuable—a man could die without either of them. Stealing a man's horse was a hanging offense. In fact, thievery in general had egregious consequences; cattle thieves were routinely hanged at the end of a rope. Men lived and died by this unwritten code of honor called the *Code of the West*.

> Chronicled by the famous western writer, Zane Grey, in his 1934 novel *The Code of the West*, no "written" code ever actually existed. However, the hardy pioneers who lived in the west were bound by these unwritten rules that centered on hospitality, fair play, loyalty, and respect for the land.[2]

Western historian Ramon Adams explains the unfolding of these laws in his 1969 book, *The Cowman and His Code of Ethics*:

> Back in the days when the cowman with his herds made a new frontier, there was no law on the range. Lack of written law made it necessary for him to frame some of his own, thus developing a rule of behavior which became known as the "Code of the West." These homespun laws, being merely a gentleman's agreement to certain rules of conduct for survival, were never written into statutes, but were respected everywhere on the range.[3]

I read an article recently about a modern-day cowboy named Waldo Wilcox. Wilcox was a rancher and mountain-lion trapper who raised cattle in the remote central Utah country from the 1950s through the end of the twentieth century. Since raising cattle was tough and financially difficult, he used his cowboy skills in other ingenious ways to augment his income. One way was to capture mountain lions and sell them to zoos. He and his dogs would corner a mountain lion out on a tree limb or a rock ledge, where Wilcox would "unlimber his lariat, lasso the lion, truss it up, and then somehow carry it down the mountain without getting mauled."[4]

Another time he single-handedly roped a stray bison that had wandered onto his land and castrated it to prevent interbreeding with his cattle:

> "I did everything wrong," Wilcox recalled, "and it all worked out right. I threw at his head and missed. He stepped in the lasso with his two front feet. I jerked the rope up and hit him sideways with my horse and he lit on his back in the wash. He couldn't get up. My horse kept the rope tight. I got down in the wash and did my business, then I let him loose. Never did see that buffalo again."
>
> For sport he roped a black bear or two ("If you give him a little slack, he'll pull the noose off with his arms, just like a monkey"), and, once, a bighorn sheep, just because when his dad had done the same thing back in the 1930s, it had made the newspapers. Nobody in Utah had ever heard of a cowboy pulling off such a stunt.[5]

Waldo Wilcox lived the Code of the West. He didn't abide by thieves or men who didn't live up to their word. He protected the wilderness that he loved and was a good steward of its history. He was tough and self-reliant (anyone who can rope and hog-tie a mountain lion has my respect). He embodied the mettle and adventurous spirit that made our country great. Waldo Wilcox is the kind of man I would like to know and hang out with if for no other reason than to hear his stories. If judged just on his performance, he strikes me as a real "man's man."

Some of the character traits valued most by cowboys included minding your own business, consideration for others, modesty, courage, perseverance, and self-sufficiency. The Code of the West required a man to be tough but generous toward others.

One of my favorite photographs is of me as a young boy wearing a fringed cowboy shirt, sitting next to Sky King. Remember Sky King, the pilot rancher who captured bad guys and spies and rescued people lost in the Arizona desert? At the beginning of his television show as his Cessna airplane, the *Songbird*, roared past, the announcer shouted, "Out of the clear blue of the western sky comes . . . Sky King!" Like many of the television cowboys of the 1950s, Sky King lived by a code. He always stood on the side of good against evil and injustice; he protected women and children; he was a bold man of action but never harmed anyone needlessly; and he was strong, smart, and competent—self-sufficient.

As men, we could do worse than to imitate the Code of the West in our lives today.

Christian Code

In the animal kingdom, the physically dominant male gets the privilege of mating with all the females. This was true for humankind as well prior to changes to civilization brought on primarily by the effects of the Christian belief system. Christianity redefined masculinity. However, now our culture seems to be sliding back the scale of acceptable masculine traits to a more base moral foundation.

The Christian honor code requires a "real" man to be faithful to and follow the Ten Commandments. He doesn't lie, cheat, steal, kill (physically, emotionally, or psychologically), or betray his wife. He honors his parents, he doesn't covet and envy things that don't belong to him, he honors and obeys God, and he doesn't worship other idols (money, material goods). Seems simple enough, doesn't it? However, as we all know, it never has been and probably never will be simple or easy.

THE TEN COMMANDMENTS

1. You shall not worship any other idol but God.
2. You shall not make a graven image.
3. You shall not take the name of God in vain.
4. You shall not break the Sabbath.
5. You shall not dishonor your parents.
6. You shall not murder.
7. You shall not commit adultery.
8. You shall not steal.
9. You shall not commit perjury.
10. You shall not covet.

Conclusion

Without honor a man's life is shallow and empty of purpose. Find a noble honor code you can live by. I found that the Christian code gave my life meaning and nobility. An honor code gives you guidelines to follow and guardrails to protect you from running off the path of life. Without these "rules of life," a man is left to weigh individual decisions on a case by case basis. This means that you will be more likely to compromise during times of struggle than you will during times of plenty.

For instance, would you sell your vote for $50? Most men probably would not. But would you sell your vote for $50,000? Now the stakes are higher. What about if you were out of work and your kids were hungry? Now the stakes are really high. Most men probably wouldn't have an affair with an average-looking woman if she approached him. But what if a supermodel or a gorgeous, famous actress approached you—would that up the stakes at all?

When we arrived at a restaurant the other day, I found a purse in the parking lot. I turned it in to the manager without thinking about it much, even though it had over $300 in cash inside. Three hundred dollars cash was not worth sacrificing my honor and integrity over. Then my wife told me about a man who found a bag containing $185,000! I wondered if I would have had as much integrity with *that* amount of money if I knew no one would ever know about it. I'd like to think so, but it's an interesting situation to think about nonetheless.

Or how about the scenario presented in the movie *Indecent Proposal*? Would you let your wife sleep with another man for a million dollars? Some men joke that *they* would have sex with the guy for a million dollars, but we need to seriously think about these kinds of moral and ethical choices before we are faced with them. Temptations seldom occur when we are best prepared to resist them. They have a way of sneaking up on us and attacking unexpectedly.

Having an established code of honor in place with people who hold us accountable to that code keeps us from making choices we will regret later. When we have a "line in the sand" that we know we won't cross, it means we don't have to have any moral ambiguity about the choices we are faced with. Having a code of honor keeps us from using situational ethics or being influenced by our emotions instead of a set of principles. Men who fall into one of those two traps make decisions they wish had never been made. Those decisions end up hurting not just us but other people as well.

5

Secondhand Lions

Coaching

Never play cards with a man called Doc. Never eat at a place called Mom's. Never sleep with a woman whose troubles are worse than your own.

Nelson Algren, *A Walk on the Wild Side*

THE ABOVE QUOTATION, while secular in nature, contains some compelling advice nonetheless. At the very least it is the author's attempt to pass along to younger men some wisdom he has learned from experience. Algren says this about his novel: "The book asks why lost people sometimes develop into greater human beings than those who have never been lost in their whole lives."[1] It's an interesting question in that we sometimes see people from horrible childhoods who turn out to be wonderful, productive citizens.

Conversely, we see kids from great homes who turn out to be criminals or at the very least make poor decisions throughout life. But the fact is that boys who do not have positive male role models face significant disadvantages as men.

In nature young mammals must be taught by their parent(s) and other mentors the skills necessary to survive. They teach those skills through modeling behaviors over and over again until the young have assimilated those behaviors. Without that training, they perish. A young bear, elk, or cougar dies quickly without a parent around. Our young people are the same way. Without proper training on how to succeed in life, they make choices that cause them and their offspring to perish rather than thrive.

I am convinced that the greatest, most effective way we help other people is through mentoring. Being mentored or guided by positive role models is also the best way that people, especially boys, learn. Males are extremely visual, and so the need to actually see an example is imperative to our learning and development process.

All males need older males to guide them through life. It is the natural order of things. Young boys look up to middle school boys for guidance on how to act. Middle school boys look up to high school boys, high school boys look up to college-age young men, and college-age young men look up to their slightly older counterparts. In fact, at all stages of life we need mentors. Young fathers need older fathers to help with questions and problems. *What did you do when your kids did this? How do I handle all the pressures and responsibilities of leading a family? Did you ever go through these challenges with your marriage?* Even older males whose children are grown and gone look up to others. I need a retired man to tell me and show me how to approach the next stage of my life now that my kids are gone. *What will life look like? What kind of challenges will my marriage face? What can I expect from my body, and what health issues will arise?*

Oftentimes we don't even realize we are looking for guidance from an older male. This again is the natural order of things. If we have good role models to follow, then we naturally tend to make good decisions and choices in life. With poor role models, however, we tend to make unhealthy or even destructive choices. The advice we get and examples set for us are those we tend to emulate.

My brother-in-law Scott is one of the most successful voice actors in Hollywood—probably at the top of his field. I noticed that Scott had grown up with several other men who are still his good friends today. Of interest to me is that all of these men are very successful in their fields of endeavor. For instance, one man is part owner of a rapidly growing national trucking company and another is a successful movie producer. They are all good men with healthy, happy marriages and families.

I asked Scott one day why he thought that all of the men in the specific group of friends he had grown up with were so successful today. It seems fairly rare that one boy out of a group of friends attains the kind of success in life that these men have had, much less that all of them have. It's not so much that they are each materially successful that's so impressive as it is that they are such good men with such good marriages and families.

Scott said something in his reply that I found to be very interesting: the biggest reason was that they were all raised by a group of good, involved fathers and other male mentors within the church they attended. They were all taught, encouraged, and held accountable by a group of men. Bingo! It's that simple.

Every man who has succeeded at anything has had a mentor or group of mentors in his life. No man, despite his protests to the contrary, is self-made. We've all had help along the way. If we have good help, it influences us one direction; if we have bad help, it steers us in another.

Boys and young men also need to be tested as part of the maturation process. Young men who never test themselves against life never find out what they are made of. They never become confident and secure in their manhood. Trials mature a man in ways that books or lectures never can. If boys are rescued (typically by female mentors) too often growing up, they never learn self-reliance and the skills to succeed in life. Most often, a boy needs a man to help teach him to navigate his way through the brambles and thornbushes of manhood. Without that guidance, too many young boys and men grow up angry, frustrated, anxious, and scared. Too often they compensate for that by exhibiting a false sense of bravado and self-confidence. I remember as a young man being angry, defensive, and brash as a way to cover my insecurities.

The truth is, if we continue to produce greater and greater numbers of angry young men, we will eventually experience an apocalyptic meltdown within our culture.

Like Father, Like Son

What we men share is the experience of having been raised by women in a culture that stopped our fathers from being close enough to teach us how to be men, in a world in which men were discouraged from talking about our masculinity and questioning its roots and its mystique, in a world that glorified masculinity and gave us impossibly unachievable myths of masculine heroics, but no domestic models to teach us how to do it.

Frank Pittman, *Man Enough*

What happens to boys and their masculinity without proper training? How and why do certain "generational cycles" get passed from one generation to the next? Children are often preprogrammed to exhibit certain tendencies or make specific choices merely by what was modeled for them when they were growing up. Traumatic events during childhood are especially ingrained in a child's psyche. Old programming, just like old habits, dies hard.

I know men who are in prison—men who are alcoholics, sex addicts, or abusive in their actions—who swore they would *never* make the same choices that their fathers made,

EFFECTS OF FATHERLESSNESS ON BOYS

- Fatherless children have more emotional and behavioral problems.
- Children from fatherless homes are five times more likely to be poor, and ten times more likely to be extremely poor than kids from homes with fathers.
- As many as 70 percent of long-term prison inmates come from homes without a father (my surveys show that if you include inmates with a "poor father figure," that percentage increases to nearly nine out of every ten men in prison).
- Children from fatherless homes are two times more likely to be high school dropouts.
- Girls from fatherless homes are three times as likely to be unwed teenage mothers (in mother-only families, adolescents are more likely to be sexually active and daughters are more likely to become single mothers).
- Boys from fatherless homes have higher incidents of unemployment, incarceration, and noninvolvement with their own children.
- 90 percent of all homeless and runaway children are from fatherless homes.
- Three out of four teen suicides are from fatherless homes.

73

and yet they are almost powerless to keep from following in the generational footsteps laid out before them. It is because those behaviors programmed into our subconscious come out when we least expect them to. Generally, despite our best intentions, our children mimic the worst of the characteristics we model for them instead of our best. I was always afraid to have a son, since I knew the potential I had to destroy him because of my background.

I had a horribly eye-opening experience the other day that illustrates clearly how this happens. When I was growing up, any time I helped my stepfather with a chore, it was a grueling experience. He was overly critical of everything I did, and most of our activities together degenerated into him yelling at me and me getting frustrated and discouraged. As a result, when my son was growing up, I unconsciously became critical at best and verbally abusive at worst (even though I told myself over and over again that I wouldn't) every time we worked together on a project. It literally was as if, despite my most stringent efforts at willpower, I could not stop myself from replaying that tape that was running through my head and had been programmed in me as a youth.

Now my son is grown and living on his own. The other day I was over at his apartment helping him install a washer and dryer. As we worked together at this simple chore, I found him snipping and harping at me for no reason, in much the same way I had been with him as he grew up. Finally, under my breath, I unconsciously made a very crude comment about my son.

He instantly yelled at me, "Don't ever call me that again in my own house!" At that point I told him I didn't have to put up with his attitude and left.

Truthfully, I did not even know I had made such a horrendous comment to him. It was not until later when I got over my own anger and recalled our entire conversation that I realized I had in fact made that comment—unconsciously mimicking like a parrot in a cage what my stepfather had said to me. I immediately returned to his house and asked for forgiveness. I explained to him that those words were an old tape that plays in my head, and when I am not consciously on guard, it rears its ugly head and spews its poison from one generation to the next.

Do I feel that way about my son? Absolutely not! I think he is a wonderful young man whom God has great plans for and will use mightily. I love him more than life itself—I would gladly die for him. And yet, I made soul-damaging comments to him without even knowing I was doing it. The part that frightens me is finally realizing that my stepfather probably acted that way toward me because that was how his father treated him. He passed that venomous bile on to me and now me to my son. It contaminates our bloodline like waste oil dripping in pure, fresh water.

And if his actions during our project are any indication, my son will eventually treat his son that way when they work together. *Dear Lord, please help me break this generational cycle so that I do not have to witness my son hurt my grandson the way I have hurt him!* My heart will shatter into pieces if I see that happen and know I was the cause, even if inadvertently.

My son and I are now having long discussions about the propensity he will have to follow in whatever negative footsteps I leave for him and how he must guard himself against this evil snare.

Recently, I asked my son to help me change our hot water heater. Given my past behavior, I was determined to remain conscious of the potential for destructive and negative comments to surface. Because I remained alert to the legacy I carried within me, I was able to control it and the words that came out of my mouth. We actually had a very good time working together and completed the project in a most satisfactory manner.

I'm still not perfect, but I am trying to consciously break that generational curse that has haunted our lineage for years.

When fathers abuse or abandon sons, their sons repeat those same behaviors with others—not always, but often. Even though they desperately might not want to, they almost cannot help imitating what was modeled for them. (If you are a man who *has* stopped those patterns, you are a cycle breaker and should know you are a mighty man!)

But direct intervention in their lives by positive male role models can make a difference. Fathers are the best ones to intervene, but nearly any man will do in a pinch. Do you know that as men we can heal wounded boys just by spending time with them, by caring about them, by investing ourselves in them, by sharing our masculine "essence" with them? It's one of the powers that God gave to men—we can fix broken boys just by spending time with them. And usually we don't even have to do anything special. Oftentimes it is just letting a boy stand next to us and watch what we do and how we do it that spreads spackle into the rip in his soul, healing the tear. Many times when a boy from divorce reaches teenage years, he starts acting out. Mom can't control him anymore, so she sends him to live with his dad or to the farm to live with grandpa. Boys instinctively know they need that male influence in their lives. They may even subconsciously act out in order to force getting sent to live with their fathers or being put in another masculine environment.

I have a friend who went on a field trip with his daughter's third grade class. On the bus ride to their destination, a little boy he had never met before came up and sat down in the seat next to him. The boy engaged him in conversation the entire trip. After arriving at the site of the field trip, the boy continued to walk and talk with my friend, eventually reaching out and taking hold of his hand while they strolled down the sidewalk. On the bus ride back to school, the boy again sat next to my friend. Halfway home, he laid his little head on my friend's shoulder and said earnestly, "I wish you were my daddy. Do you wish I was your son?"

My friend related this story to me with tears in his eyes. The yearning and craving this boy had for masculine "essence" was overwhelming. He was like a dry sponge soaking up my friend's maleness.

Walking Tall (While Standing)

Fat, drunk, and stupid is no way to go through life, son.

Dean Vernon Wormer, *Animal House*

Several years ago we began presenting seminars for women on raising boys to become good men. We found a huge segment of our culture where women were being forced to raise sons on their own. Many of these women faced big disadvantages raising boys and understanding what their sons needed not only by not being male themselves but by not having been raised with a father or brothers while growing up. In response to their dilemma of not having positive male role models for their sons, we started a program called Standing Tall. Standing Tall is a mentoring program for fatherless boys. It is similar to a faith-based Big Brothers program. It originally started in partnership with a local Bible college. There we trained male seminary students to spend a couple of hours a week with fatherless boys who were identified through our seminars for moms. Almost immediately we started seeing some startling results. Mothers of the boys began reporting that their sons' entire countenances were changing. They reported that their sons were better behaved, less angry, and doing better in school. Some even credited the presence of the mentors with their sons' improvement in reading scores (even though they never read together) and behavioral changes such as cessation of bedwetting. Nearly all of the boys experienced more self-confidence and composure during their daily-life activities.

We encourage the mentors to use physical activities with the boys. Many fatherless boys spend large amounts of un-supervised time in front of the television or video games, which is unhealthy on a lot of different levels. We also en-courage "teaching" opportunities. Things such as how to drive a nail, catch a baseball, shoot basketball hoops, ride a bike, use a pocketknife safely, hike in the wilderness, and so on—all the things that boys without dads do not learn and therefore feel inadequate because of. If the boys are older, we sometimes teach them skills such as shaving and other appropriate personal hygiene tips. You might be surprised at the simplest things you and I take for granted that fatherless boys do not know how to do. And because it is embarrassing to ask, they often stumble through life without ever getting that knowledge.

Once while I was speaking at a prison, one of the inmates told me a powerful story of how this affects males even after they have grown into adulthood. He told me that his cell mate was a very large, angry, and frightening man with a full beard. One morning he awoke to the sound of someone sobbing. He opened his eyes to see this cell mate attempting to dry shave his full beard with a disposable razor. He very cautiously asked his cell mate what was wrong. His cell mate turned toward him, and he saw that he had cut his cheek very deeply attempting to shave. He was bleeding profusely down his front and on the sink.

"What are you doing?" he asked.

"I'm shaving!" the man said angrily.

Very tentatively, the man asked, "Why are you shaving that way?"

"Because I never had a father and no one ever taught me how!" the man shouted in frustration.

Here was a man who had never been shown the most basic of masculine hygiene. He covered it by growing a beard. When he did attempt to learn a new skill, he was humiliated. The man told me that he offered to show his cell mate how to shave. The cell mate was so grateful that he nearly started crying again.

We also encourage intentionally teaching character traits such as self-discipline, perseverance (not quitting), honesty, courage, respect for women (mother), and others. Many of these boys do not learn these character traits, not because the mother doesn't value them, but because they are more readily learned and accepted coming from another male.

Other issues that we observe in fatherless boys are the unwillingness to accept challenges. Because they have no confidence and a reluctance to experience humiliation through their failures, many of these boys do not receive the valuable lessons and self-esteem of failing and persevering until they succeed. They also become frustrated and quit anything the first time it becomes difficult. They tend to cry easier than most boys. Very often they have been feminized by having only female influences in their lives. They come to expect to be "rescued" by mom (or another female) and frequently will not try new things. In fairness to them, they don't know any better—Mom has always rescued them. As they become older, they get indecisive, passive, docile, and unable to commit to a relationship. They tend to rely on females to make all the decisions that govern their lives and seldom take on natural leadership roles. When they fall down and scrape a knee, they will instantly cry and wait for Mom to come and rescue them. If a man picks them up and dusts them off, they recognize they are not really hurt and stop crying right away. Again a male's presence helps to guide and encourage them to persevere until they succeed, thereby gaining the positive self-image and confidence to accept risk and attempt challenges in other areas of life.

These boys are also often angry. Sometimes their anger is externalized and apparent in social and educational venues, and other times it is internalized in passive-aggressive behavior. Frankly, they have a right to be angry—they have been deprived of their God-given right to a father who will teach them how to make their way in this big, harsh world. They do not have a father to teach, protect, and empathize with their struggles. Frequently, though, this anger is being used to cover other emotions such as fear, humiliation, anxiety, vulnerability, or even pain. Unless these boys are taught to recognize this, they are doomed to believe they can solve any problem in life by using anger and other unhealthy coping mechanisms.

And they often feel bad about themselves. Here's how Donald Miller describes feeling as a boy growing up without a father: "I wondered if people who grow up with great fathers don't walk around with a subconscious sense they are wanted on this planet, that they belong, and the world needs them. . . . In life, there were people who were meant to live and people who were accidently born, elected to plod the globe as the despised."[2]

Another observation we make about fatherless boys is the propensity they all have to be somewhat "off" or "different." They tend to have trouble fitting in—probably because of lack of a male role model. Many (if not most) seem to have some sort of disadvantage associated with them. It might consist of behavioral problems, speech impediments, emotional struggles, or even learning disabilities (frequently ADHD); but they generally have some sort of physical or emotional "issue" that sets them apart from their peers. Often these differences cause them to be isolated and more comfortable in female company, which is more compassionate and accepting.

These observations are purely anecdotal, but various studies appear to support the emotional struggles of fatherless boys. The trauma and stress of losing their father, possibly combined with having only female influences in their lives, manifests itself through a variety of problems.

In a study described in the book *Destructive Trends in Mental Health: The Well-Intentioned Path to Harm* by Rogers Wright and Nicholas Cummings, kids with ADHD were paired with male therapists due to a noted absence of father involvement in the children's lives. The kids were given behavioral treatment with the therapists, and special attention was paid to developing a positive attachment to the male figure. At the end of the treatment, only 11 percent of the boys and 2 percent of the girls had to remain on medication. The authors of this study suggested that social forces may be major contributors to ADHD. Among these social forces are "the absence of positive father role models; the presence of a revolving door for negative male role models brought into the home; poor parenting; the need for order in the classroom when teachers are severely curtailed in meting out discipline; and a declining appreciation in our culture of what constitutes normal boy behavior."[3]

I frequently receive emails from mothers or relatives of boys who struggle mightily because they lack male role models. These boys have any number of problems, but it's pretty obvious that all of their troubles begin and end with the loss of their father. The path placed before them gives them little chance of successfully living a healthy life. We have found the best, perhaps only, way to break this destructive cycle is to educate the mother on healthy masculine traits and then introduce a positive male role model in the boy's life.

Our intention is to take the Standing Tall program to churches and colleges around the country where men, young and old alike, can help change the lives of boys who otherwise have the deck stacked against them.

Coaching

> Coaching is making men do what they don't want, so they
> can become what they want to be.
>
> Tom Landry

The movie *Coach Carter* is based on a true story. In 1999, former high school standout basketball player and successful businessman Ken Carter returned to coach at Richmond High School in Richmond, California. Carter took a losing inner-city program of young men programmed to fail in life and turned them into winners—at basketball and at life. He instantly began working on their self-respect and respect for others. He had the players sign a contract saying that they would maintain a 2.3 grade point average, attend all classes, sit in the front row of each class, and wear ties and jackets to school on game days.

After winning their first sixteen games of the season, Coach Carter was disillusioned to discover that many of the young men were failing academically and not attending classes. They had failed to honor their end of the agreement. He locked the gym and canceled practice, eventually forfeiting two games until all members of the team were in compliance with the contract they had signed. This made the national news because it was so rare that anyone in our culture would hold principles and values above athletic competition. But Carter understood that these young, mostly African American men had no chance to succeed in life without the hope provided by an education. They were being programmed to fail by a dysfunctional system that had given up on them. He taught them the principles of self-discipline, perseverance, and work ethic necessary to succeed in life. He taught them life lessons, not just basketball skills. He held them accountable. Like most young men, once they recognized that this older man knew what he was talking about and that he had their best interests at heart, they bought into his program. They went on to play in the state championship tournament, barely losing to the number one team in the state. At least five of the members of that team went on to attend college, several graduating.

Here was an entire group of young men destined for lives of hopelessness and failure who were given a chance at life because an older man had coached them in the skills they needed to succeed.

Perhaps the term *coaching* is a better word to use than the word *mentoring*. The concept of mentoring seems a bit intimidating to most men or seems focused on achieving career success. Mentoring also conjures up the responsibility to be some great, wise teacher who never fails and never makes mistakes. No man can live up to that expectation. And yet God has given us gifts and the power to influence lives beyond comprehension. *Coaching* seems a more natural term for most men. And what we're talking about here goes so much deeper than the business-oriented assumptions often associated with the word *mentoring*.

A coach's job is not only to teach a player the skills he needs to be successful but to motivate him to use those skills to the best of his ability. Part of the job requires getting greater performance out of team members than they can achieve on their own. A coach does that in part by believing in his players and encouraging them to push themselves out of their comfort zones for their own good. A good coach will be respected by his players because they know he has their best interests at heart. He may even be loved by his players but frequently will not be liked very well, at least off and on. That's because good coaching requires helping players look at their faults and then pushing them to accomplish things they do not think they can or even want to do.

Even Hollywood in its infinite wisdom recognizes that boys need men to inspire and lead them to greater heights. A number of excellent sports movies portray this reality very effectively, including *Remember the Titans, Hoosiers, Facing the Giants* (produced by a church, not Hollywood), and *Coach Carter.*

I once heard a man say, "My father died recently and I realized that I never really knew him. I regret that more than anything in my entire life." How many of us do not really know our fathers or our sons? What a waste not to pass along all the lessons we have learned from a lifetime of trial and error, failure and success, winning and losing at life. I certainly do not want to go to my grave never having passed along my wisdom to my children and grandchildren.

Steve Farrar talks about the fact that it is not enough to be a positive example for our sons. We have to actively coach them, even as they get older.[4]

When I read that, it was like a bighorn sheep running full speed across the face of a mountain and head butting me. I recognized that I had assumed as my son got older that just being a good role model was enough. I had stopped intentionally coaching him! I immediately asked my son to start having lunch once a week with me to study various books so that it would stimulate topics of discussion on issues he needed my input and experience on. I returned to intentionally coaching him. I am using my influence to subtly steer him in directions that are healthy and away from areas that are destructive. I am encouraging him and even pushing him a little to get out of his comfort zone. I'm coaching him in the fundamentals of how to "play" the game of life.

So what keeps us from passing this information, knowledge, and wisdom along? Is it because we think we have failed at times? That's how we learn—by failing! Those who have never failed never learn anything. And those who never try anything fail by omission. That insidious, sinister voice inside your head is telling you that you are not worthy—that you don't have anything of value to give to the next generation. It's all part of the dark side's strategy to keep older men from guiding the next generation. If we all have to keep repeating the same mistakes, we can never be effective. Not only that, but the stakes keep rising when we repeat history's failures. The problems get bigger and the consequences get more devastating.

SOME FUN THINGS THAT BOYS NEED TO BE TAUGHT BY A MAN

1. They need to learn important stuff like how to spit properly, with all the different forms of spitting and their varied nuances.
2. They need to be taught how to sharpen a knife and the importance of a sharp knife.
3. They need to know that you never point a gun at someone (even a toy gun) unless you intend to use it. They need to be taught how to properly and safely handle a gun, including how to shoot it and clean it.
4. They need to learn the proper way to chop wood and light a fire.
5. They need to be taught how to use a compass so that they know they will never be lost again.
6. They need to be taught how to throw and catch a baseball and a football.
7. They need to be taught how to fix a flat tire and change the oil in a car. And how to find and repair a leak in a bicycle tire.
8. They need to learn how to pound a nail with a hammer and drive it straight. They also need to learn how to properly saw a board.

We held a retreat at a ranch with a big, stone fireplace in the great room. Someone asked a young man from the city to build a fire in the fireplace. I saw he was struggling and casually gave him a few tips. Soon he had a majestic fire roaring in the fireplace. As people came along and complimented him on his great fire, he was quick to say, "Rick taught me how!" It was as if he was so grateful and excited that a man had taught him something handy that he couldn't wait to let everyone know. That experience built his confidence because he knows he can start a fire if he needs to. Seems like a small thing, doesn't it? But being *capable* is important to our self-esteem as men. If no one shows us how to do something, how can we ever learn to be capable? And if we do not feel capable, how can we feel good about our manhood?

I can hear half of you guys thinking, *I'm off the hook; my kids are girls.* But if you are a man who does not have any sons, just daughters, then you have an even more vested interest in making sure boys are raised to be good men. Your daughters are counting on you!

If you are a man, someone needs you. You won't have to look far to find a male younger than yourself who desperately needs what you've already learned. Open yourself to the opportunities to be used. I promise you will not regret it. The satisfaction you will get from seeing how you are helping to change lives with such very little effort on your part will be a magnificent blessing in your life. It will make you feel like a man!

6

Kelly's Heroes

A Life of Significance

WHEN HURRICANE KATRINA destroyed thousands of people's homes in the poorest sections of New Orleans, Canadian billionaire Frank Stronach wanted to help. He didn't want to just give money, so he purchased 800 acres of land about 150 miles from New Orleans and started an experimental model community called Canadaville. Canadaville consists of about 49 mobile home units. Each unit is a three-bedroom, two-bath, 1,420-square-foot single-family residence complete with furniture and central air-conditioning. Stronach donated about $8 million of his own money to purchase the land and build the residences. The residents can stay up to five years rent free as long as they follow the Character of Conduct rules, which consist of the following: each occupant must have a job or be in school, must perform eight hours a month of community service, must attend local council meetings, and must remain drug free. So far, the self-sustaining organic farming community has about 200 occupants. The goal of the community is to teach people new skills to be able to start over again. Most residents are expected to eventually return to New Orleans to pick up the pieces of their lives. When they leave, the housing units will be turned over to the Red Cross for use as emergency housing.[1]

Stronach wanted to give people a hand up, not a handout. Most of the people who have lived at Canadaville were destitute and untrained. They consider this opportunity to be a second chance at life. Frank Stronach is using his influence and leadership to make a difference in the world.

Living a life of significance and substance is a key factor to a man feeling that his life means something. Leadership is one of the birthrights of our gender. But with the privilege of leadership come greater responsibilities. By treating that responsibility conscientiously, we earn the right to be leaders in our homes and communities. But being a leader requires us to shuck off the stifling blanket of apathy and step up to the plate.

Stepping Up to the Plate

Men should speak the truth, and then allow their actions to affirm their values. The opposite of love is not hate, it is indifference. To not speak up when someone is making choices that harm themselves or others (including our children by what they watch on television or what is being sold to them by morally bankrupt corporations) is not being tolerant or somehow noble, it is being indifferent at best and cowardly

90

at worst. Clearly, judging a person is unbiblical. However, judging a person's actions is what a man who lives a life of significance does.

While growing up, my children somewhat jokingly accused me of being a bigot (although I don't think they understood the true definition of the word) because they thought I judged people too harshly—some of whom were men of color. And yet they are amazed that I have many very good friends of color, men I invite into our home, break bread with, pray with and for, and love as brothers. I try to explain to them that I judge all men individually by their character and their actions, not by their skin color or ethnicity.

That's not what our culture teaches them. Our sons and daughters have been indoctrinated by a public educational system and media culture that says my actions of judging *anything* are intolerant and racist. The truth is, any man can be a good man or a failure, regardless of his race, color, ethnicity, or religion. It doesn't take a special color or ethnicity to be less than we are capable of. If we are honest, we all know we fall short of our potential. Besides, if you've ever played sports or fought side by side in battle, you know that of all things, skin color is the least important trait by which to judge another man. But if we do not judge a man by his actions, we run the risk of allowing (even encouraging) every man to do whatever he wants, resulting in chaos and harm to innocent parties.

Victor Frankl, author of *Man's Search for Meaning*, said that even within the confines of the concentration camps during World War II he found only two types of men: decent and non-decent ones. Both types were found in all classes, ethnicities, and groups.[2]

Our silence or indifference in matters of importance can allow great harm to occur. For the past ninety years or so, the choir at one of our local high schools has put on a wonderful Christmas assembly. The songs were chosen by the students each year and performed in front of the entire school at an assembly. Generally the students chose a mix of traditional Christmas songs reflecting the true nature of the season. The songs were beautiful, and my wife says it sounded as if angels from heaven were singing God's praise. She would pray during the entire assembly for the kids who were hurting to be touched by God's love and grace. Many people were moved to tears by the voice of hope they heard.

Over the past several years, however, the school administration has been leaning heavily on the choir director to include a more diverse range of songs to include other religions and faiths (including Wiccan) and to exclude anything to do with Christ. Two years ago, the name was formally changed from Christmas Pageant to Holiday Assembly. Finally, this year, after the complaints of a couple of teachers (not students or parents, mind you) regarding the "religious" nature of the songs the students chose, the pageant was canceled and rescheduled for the spring when, as the music director stated, more "serious" literature will be performed.

I'm not sure where politically correct nonsense like this ends, and obviously my letter of protest didn't do any good. Nothing was printed in the newspaper, and this decision silently slipped through like a wisp of fog in the night. But I do know that if the principal of the school had received fifty or a hundred letters and telephone calls from men in the community strongly voicing their opinions on this issue, she would have sat up and taken notice. And this wonderful gift to students and adults alike would not have vanished. Now that it's gone, I wonder if it will ever return. Perhaps one day people will wake up and ask themselves, "What's happening to our high schools? How come the kids do so poorly and act so destructively?" Oh yeah, that's already happening.

By allowing all vestiges of a moral foundation (no prayer, no Ten Commandments, no mention of Christmas, no God) to be removed from the public forum and thus leaving nothing to build upon, we doom the next generation to confusion, frustration, and moral ambiguity.

Significance or Insignificance

The belief in a God All Powerful wise and good, is so essential to the moral order of the World and to the happiness of man.

President James Madison, November 20, 1825

If we must all die (and we must), then let's at least die knowing we lived lives of meaning—that our time here on earth stood for *something*. There is nothing more pitiful than a man faced with his own mortality who realizes he was insignificant.

In the movie *Schindler's List*, Liam Neeson stars as Oskar Schindler, a German industrialist during World War II. In an effort to capitalize on the war, he acquired a factory in Poland, which he ran with the cheapest labor around—Jewish labor.

At first he seemed like every other greedy German industrialist, driven by profit and unmoved by the means of his profiteering. But somewhere along the line, something changed. He succeeded in his quest for riches, but by the end of the war he had spent everything he made on keeping 1,100 Jewish men and women alive. He literally bought their lives.

In a powerful scene at the end of the movie, with Allied forces bearing down, Schindler said good-bye to the many Jewish factory workers he had saved. The workers had removed some of their gold-filled teeth to create a ring for Schindler. Inside the ring, they engraved an old Hebrew proverb, "Whoever saves one life, saves the world entire."

As they gave him the ring in gratitude, Schindler broke down and began sobbing in remorse. He regretted that he had not done more to save additional lives. Even when the workers tried to console him that he had done so much more than anyone else, he cried out in agony over regret at his complacency.

Schindler, while certainly not as complacent as many of us, realized too late that he could have done so much more. He regretted it dearly. And while others did not blame him, he knew in his heart that he could have done more.

When my time comes, I do not want to be a man on my knees before God with my face in my hands sobbing with regret over the fact that I did not use the gifts that God gave me to make a difference in other people's lives. That it took until then to recognize the missed opportunities and lost rewards I squandered. Personally, I think those who profess to rely solely on grace and have no compunction to do good works are spiritually (and maybe physically) lazy.

I look up to men like Bill McCartney, who started Promise Keepers, and Chuck Colson, founder of Prison Fellowship. These are heroic men who were successful in their chosen professions and yet elected to spend their powers and influence to make a difference in the world. Each of them have impacted the lives of untold thousands of people and probably will for generations to come, merely by using the gifts God gave them for something other than their own self-gratification.

We were all created uniquely and wonderfully. It is only because of the pollution from an emotionally toxic world and the contamination we receive from wounded people who are important to us that we believe ourselves less than the image of God. Every man carries the seeds of greatness within him. It is up to us to water and nurture those seeds so that we can achieve the potential God created us for.

Men, know this, no matter who you are, how young or old you are, no matter what mistakes you have made in the past—there are people out there watching you, looking up to you to see how a man lives his life. People you don't know and will never know are being influenced by how you conduct yourself and how you face life. There are people out there literally dying because of lack of positive, healthy male leadership in their lives. Women and girls, boys, and even other men are watching you to see how a man solves problems, makes decisions, and lives his life. They need you more than you will ever know. Most of us don't recognize that and waste the obligation God has given us to make a difference in the lives of those around us.

Every month I spend time at either the Oregon State Penitentiary or the state correctional institution teaching the inmates classes on fathering or authentic masculinity. People ask me all the time, "Do you really think you are doing any good speaking to men in prison? Do you think you make a difference in their lives?"

My truthful answer is, "I don't know." Many of the men do come up afterward and appear to be genuinely impacted. But it doesn't matter what I think. It's not up to me whether I make a difference or not. That is up to God. My role is as a messenger. I do the best I can to stand in the gap and leave the results in the Lord's more capable hands.

I do know this, though. Those men in prison can never say after I've spoken to them that no one ever told them how important they are in the lives of their children. Or of how much value their lives have. They may have never heard that message before in their entire lives. Someone has to tell them—if not me, then who?

Challenges

All men face challenges. Truthfully, most of us face the same challenges. How we react to those challenges separates good men from average men or even bad men.

I wrote about my friend Randy in the first chapter of this book. But I didn't give you the entire picture of the challenges he has faced. During just one year of his life, here are some of the challenges he faced. He and his wife had an unexpected pregnancy at the age of forty. They had twins, and one of the twins had Down syndrome and required open-heart surgery shortly after birth. During this time, his father-in-law died and his grief-stricken mother-in-law moved in with them. His father contracted prostate cancer, and his sister-in-law was battling ovarian cancer. Because of all this, his mother entered into a bout with severe depression. Shortly thereafter, a sexual abuse scandal erupted at the church he leads, which led to arrests and devastation for many families of the congregation.

Talk about stress! Many men might have just given up. And yet, Randy has come through all those trials as a man of wisdom, compassion, and grace, who works powerfully in the lives of many other people. Randy will tell you he is no different than any other man, but his resiliency and faith in God raised him above the struggles and trials of life to become a man who makes a difference in the world.

Everyone tells me that people need "permission" before they will attempt to change or try something new. Men, if you want to be a good man—a man of significance—you have my permission. More than that, you have my blessing. If there is anything I can do to be of help in your journey, I will do it. God created you as a magnificent beast with the power to change lives. Don't waste that gift. Nurture it and use it to bless people's lives.

I remember the first time I recognized the power of this gift. A woman came up at a seminar and tearfully told me her marriage had been saved because her husband had previously attended one of my fathering workshops.

I frequently receive letters like the one below:

Hello Rick,

I thoroughly enjoyed reading your book and have put it into practice. I've been separated from my wife and family for over 15 months now. She relocated to Atlanta from New Jersey where we previously resided.

I visited with my family (three children) during the Christmas holidays. While my older son (10 years old) and I went shopping for groceries, he noticed a book rack and picked out your book, *Better Dads, Stronger Sons*, then handed it to me. I assumed he was telling me something. I purchased it and since then I have been profoundly affected by many of the issues you brought up—both in regards to the father/son and husband/wife relationships.

I've spoken with my wife about my eyes being opened, as well as some serious praying. Prayerfully, I will be re-joining my family in Georgia by the end of summer as there are some loose ends I need to tie up here in the New York area and some job hunting that needs to be searched before I come.

With many thanks I appreciate your book.

Messages like this give me powerful motivation when times are difficult. By using the power God has given you to touch other people's lives, you will find a whole world out there that will honor your efforts and make you feel like a "real" man.

But God can't steer a parked bus. In other words, we need to be *doing* something in order for God to work in our lives. Well, obviously, God can do whatever he wants and does perform miracles every day. But as a rule, he never forces us to do anything. I think for most of us average guys, God tends to work in our lives in a more pragmatic way based upon our faith, perseverance, and hard work. When we prepare ourselves beforehand, then take action, it allows God to direct us more easily toward the path he established for our lives.

Unfortunately, we oftentimes do not see the bigger picture like God does. Frequently God gives us information on a "need to know" basis. When the angel visited Mary, he told her only that she would be pregnant with the Son of God. He neglected to tell her that her son would later be crucified—it wasn't something she needed to know in order to fulfill the role God had planned for her.

But it brings up an interesting point, in that service for the Lord often has a cost associated with it. Mary's cost was her reputation. Many men throughout history have suffered the loss of everything from their reputations, to their families, to their lives in service of God. When we decide to allow God to use us, we must be aware of the cost and be willing to pay the price. The greater the potential for significance, the greater the risks (and cost) associated with it.

Interestingly, God most often uses men like you and me who are not perfect, who make mistakes and fail, because it proves his existence. Frankly, I do things every day (such as writing books and speaking in front of large groups) that I am not qualified or capable of doing on my own—in reality, I'm scared to death. God chooses average, flawed men to do his will. Jesus didn't pick the same kind of men that the world would have chosen as his disciples. He picked ordinary men with obvious faults and made them into something extraordinary through the indwelling of the Holy Spirit.

When I first became a Christian, I had a strong desire to do *something* of significance for the Lord. My life had seemed pretty insignificant up until that point. I had a successful business and a lovely wife and great children, but there was a vacuum in my soul that needed to be filled. My life felt unsatisfying and meaningless.

So I prayed consistently for several years that God would show me what he had in store. But during that time, I also kept in motion, trying different activities—such as ushering at church, picketing abortion clinics, and attending men's groups—in order to find out what my gifts were and what areas God wanted to use me in most effectively. I also continued to improve myself personally by reading books and attending conferences. Over a period of time God helped me see what he wanted me to do by the doors that he opened and the opportunities he placed in my path. However, this required me to take some risks, to be bold and have courage in stretching myself and going out of my comfort zone in many areas. God wants to stretch us, to test our mettle. When we take those kinds of risks, it confirms the level of our faith in God, certainly to others, perhaps even to him. I don't pretend to know how God thinks and acts, but I do know that it seemed as if I had to endure a certain amount of trials and tribulations, have my faith tested, and learn a magnitude of lessons before God started to use me effectively and consistently.

God did not give me all the information about what he had in store for me beyond an intial vision that was just the tip of the iceberg. Had he given more information than I needed, I probably would not have been willing to go through with it—it might have seemed overwhelming. He has given me just enough relevant information on a "need to know" basis to continue down the path he set before me.

My wife and I have had to pay the price of being used by God. I was sued, lost my business, nearly lost our home, and spent all of our savings and retirement to survive while starting this ministry. Sometimes that price seems enormous and other times it seems insignificant. Nevertheless, a price has been paid that has changed me forever.

A Man's Obligations

On September 11, 2001, United Flight 93 left New Jersey headed for San Francisco. Shortly after takeoff, the flight was hijacked by five Islamic terrorists who killed the pilot, copilot, and one of the flight attendants. After hearing that three other commercial airliners had been hijacked and crashed into the

World Trade Center buildings and the Pentagon, the remaining crew and passengers took matters into their own hands. Rather than sit quietly and be victims of evil, they rushed the terrorists, which resulted in the plane being crashed in a vacant field in rural Pennsylvania.

The passengers and crew of United Flight 93 were real-life heroes. They willingly sacrificed their lives for the lives of others and for the sake of their fellow countrymen. They took action in the face of evil.

I believe that because I am a man, my obligation in life is to help others. To lift them up to be what they could not attain without my presence in their lives. I choose to walk a nobler path in life than the path that our culture dictates a man should walk. And if my efforts should be in vain? Well, then at least I failed while daring greatly.

Instead of sitting around complaining, we men need to get up and *do* something. Even if our contributions are minor, they are important. They may seem minor to us, but we never know their full impact now and for generations to come. I know it sometimes seems overwhelming for one man to try to make a difference in this world. But if enough people do small things, they add up to major changes. One small candle may not make much difference in a dark auditorium, but a hundred lit candles make a huge difference. What might seem minor to us often has a life-changing effect on others—just ask a boy who has been given sorely needed advice or encouragement by a man. I often meet people who tell me that another person told them something that literally changed their lives. When I ask the source about it, they frequently don't even remember making the statement. We never know who is watching us and looking to us for leadership. It is our responsibility—our obligation—to be the best leaders we can be. Part of making a difference is sharing ourselves with others so that they can benefit from our experiences and hard-earned wisdom. When we change one life, we potentially change thousands of lives. In fact, change one life and you change the world.

A Life of Significance

Men have this innate desire to do something significant. But many times we press it down and repress the desire. The husband of a friend of mine was recently diagnosed with terminal cancer. The first words out of his mouth after hearing the diagnosis were, "What have I accomplished of significance with my life?" Stunned, he repeatedly moaned it over and over again as the realization of his diagnosis sunk in.

Think about that! His first thought during the shock of finding out he was to die early in life was a regret over his lack of significance. Unfortunately, this man did not understand that he had led a true life of significance by being a good husband and father. He raised not only a daughter but also a stepdaughter as his own, both to fine young womanhood.

We grow up hearing phrases like "men of honor," "men of integrity," "a man's man," and "a man among men." We throw these sayings around but don't really think about what they mean in our lives. Does not every man aspire to this kind of greatness? I don't know any man who wouldn't want to be known as a "man among men." Early on in life we crave this kind of title, and as we get older and more timid we lose the vision. Our fear of failure and rejection grows enough to make us crave safety and keep us from striving for greatness; and when we do so, we settle for mediocrity. By not rocking the boat and risking failure, we sacrifice our chance for greatness.

The Bible speaks about our responsibility to be salt and light to a hurting world. Light provides many things. First of all, it is a metaphor for God's grace and wisdom. Without accepting those gifts of light, we are forced to stumble through life in the dark. We are not able to see potential hazards beforehand. We do not see the cliff in front of us. The power of a candle lights our way along the path of life. Light also provides protection—in the woods, fire keeps predators at bay. Fire gives us warmth. It even preserves life if things get too cold.

But the power of light also forces us to examine our faults. If we are in the dark, we do not have to face those faults, either because we cannot see them or they are more easily ignored.

As men, we *must*, individually and as a collective gender, rise up and confront the social crises of our times. Our dereliction of duty in giving our children our time, physical affection, and love has resulted in drugs and alcohol abuse, sexual promiscuity, eating disorders, self-mutilation, and various other self-abuses our children use to fill the vacuum we have left in their souls. Our mission is to right wrongs and fight worthy battles—and there are plenty of those to go around. We must develop a vision of masculinity for ourselves, for young men, and for boys that will inspire us and them to strive for greatness instead of settling for mediocrity.

Symbols of Significance

All men have a yearning for greatness, for significance. We want to know we came from a noble heritage or lineage.

My great-grandfather, Olaf Landsverk, immigrated to this country from Norway as a teenager. Because we come from a Scandinavian bloodline, my son likes to think he is descended from Vikings. He likes the thrill of believing that our ancestors were once mighty warriors.

But it's not just boys who revel in these kinds of dreams. My dad told of seeing photos of Olaf in a US Army uniform with a sword as a veteran of the Spanish-American War. I experienced a rush of excitement when my dad said that it was rumored that Olaf was one of Teddy Roosevelt's Rough Riders. I seemed to walk a little taller and prouder believing that one of my ancestors was linked to greatness in some way.

Symbols also seem to be important to men. We value medals awarded for deeds of great courage and valor. We treasure trophies for competitive accomplishments. Scars are a boy's medals—his sign of toughness worthy of bragging rights. Symbols say, "You were here—you meant something."

One day my father gave me a magnificent gift and symbol. He formally handed over my great-grandfather Olaf's hunting rifle. Olaf had used this rifle to hunt deer and perhaps protect his family in the backwoods of northern Wisconsin. It had been passed down by my grandfather Frank and after him my uncle Bob. After Uncle Bob passed away, my father inherited this treasured heirloom.

The rifle is a model 1894 Marlin .25/.36, with an octagonal barrel. It weights about ten pounds, and has no safety. After I received it, I had it professionally cleaned and the firing pin replaced. I've been offered upwards of $1200 for it, but I wouldn't sell it for any price. It's probably not powerful enough to drop one of the big "muleys" (mule deer) that we hunt in eastern Oregon. Even though it's impractical, heavy, and a little dangerous, I always take it when I go hunting and carry it at least one day of the hunt. My dream is to at least once use it to put food on my table like the men of my lineage have for generations.

This rifle is a mighty, valorous, battle-scarred weapon passed down from father to son for generations, and I treasure it with all my heart. Someday I will pass it on to be entrusted to the care of my son for future generations in our legacy.

And so a man's life can be passed down like a valorous symbol from one generation to the next. How will your grandsons and great-grandsons remember your legacy? Will you be a forgotten man—or will your legacy be one of significance? One passed down from father to son that makes the male receiving it feel proud and excited to have that bloodline coursing through his veins. One that says you made the world a better place because you were here.

I tell men who mentor fatherless boys that they may never see the results of their efforts here on earth. But someday in heaven, multitudes of people they have never met before will approach them in gratitude for the gift of themselves that they gave to another human, which in some way touched and changed their lives as well. It will be a wonderful and exciting way to spend eternity—knowing that you made a difference!

7

The Magnificent Seven (Plus One)

TRAITS

I looked for a man among them who would build up the wall and stand before me in the gap on behalf of the land so I would not have to destroy it, but I found none.

Ezekiel 22:30–31 NIV

NEARLY EVERY MAN I've spoken with about masculinity talks about the importance of character and integrity in reference to what makes a man. Clearly certain character traits have defined masculinity since the beginning of time. Have those traits changed in recent years, or are the ones that spoke to our great-great-grandfathers' souls still what matter most to manhood?

Michael Vick, star quarterback of the Atlanta Falcons, had a multimillion-dollar contract and millions of dollars more in commercial endorsements. He had everything life had to offer and a brilliant future ahead of him. In December 2007, Vick was sentenced to twenty-three months in prison for funding and operating a dog fighting operation on one of his properties. Not only that, but he admitted (after initially lying about it) that he participated in the killing of dogs that did not perform well in the ring. Including salary, incentives, and endorsements, Vick stands to lose more than $140 million. A gifted athlete, any potential future in professional football is now in question. His reputation will always be tainted, and his failure to live up to his potential will scar his legacy.

Contrast that with his teammate, running back Warrick Dunn. Dunn is the founder of the Warrick Dunn Foundation, a not-for-profit organization. One of the foundation's key programs is the Homes for the Holidays program. The Homes for the Holidays program assists single-parent families in realizing the dream of first-time home ownership by providing down payment assistance on a house and furnishing it with everything a first-time homeowner would need, including furniture, food, linens, lawn mower, gardening supplies, washer, dryer, dishes, pots and pans, and so forth.

The oldest of six children, Warrick grew up watching his mother, Betty Smothers, provide for him and his five siblings. As a single mother, she worked endless hours as a Baton Rouge police officer and at several off-duty jobs to make ends meet. During Warrick's senior year of high school, his mother's life was taken in the line of duty, leaving him the responsibility of keeping the family together. Although she worked hard all of her life, Betty was never able to realize the American Dream of owning her own home.

Dunn says of his childhood, "I was blessed to have people in my life who taught me the importance of helping others in need. I did not grow up with many material things, but I was surrounded by the love of my family, friends, and coaches. My mother worked overtime to put food on the table and a roof over our heads. Although we did not have much, she taught me how to give of myself and to be generous to those in need."

The program honors his mother's dream of home ownership for other single mothers. As of the end of 2007, the Homes for the Holidays program had assisted seventy-three single moms achieve first-time home ownership.

Warrick Dunn is using his character to guide him in making a significant difference in the world. He is helping others by changing their lives and possibly their destinies. His legacy will be one of hope and significance.

Activities like sports and military service that require self-discipline tend to build character in young men. Under the authority and tutelage of older men who teach, mentor, coach, and push them beyond their limits, these young men find out who they are and what they are made of. Done properly (emphasis on *properly*), this develops self-esteem and a confidence born of trial and error that stays with them for a lifetime. I carry with me today many of the lessons I

CHARACTERISTICS OF A MAN AS DESCRIBED BY OTHER MEN

Rugged
Handles (internalizes) physical pain
Doesn't quit easily
Competent and capable
Inspires others
Leadership
Visionary
Courageous
Dependable
Passionate
Action-oriented
Faithful
Calmness in crisis
Humility
Confidence
Vitality
Intensity
Makes those under his protection and leadership feel safe

learned in sports and from my coaches (at least the good ones), traits like perseverance (not quitting when times were tough), teamwork, the value of hard work, and respect for my teammates, rules, and those in authority. In addition, I matured a lot as a man during my tour on active duty in the military.

Are traits like competitiveness primal in some or all males? Competitiveness seems to be a common characteristic in most men and in most cultures. All men appear to have some sort of drive to make their mark in the world. Men who do not compete directly against other men usually compete against themselves. Fathers and sons generally have some sort of competitive rivalry against each other where the son cannot achieve manhood until he comes out from under the father's shadow. Even so-called sensitive males are competitive. Chess matches and musical competitions can be every bit as intense and competitive as anything on the basketball court or football field.

There are a number of common character traits that we typically associate with men, such as being bold and assertive. During the battle of Thermopylae in 480 BC, a small Greek force led by 300 Spartans held off a huge Persian army of between 300,000 and a million men. The reported words of a Persian spoken before the battle are, "Our arrows will blot out the sun!" to which a Spartan replies, "Then we will fight in the shade." That seemed like a pretty bold proclamation in the face of overwhelming adversity to me, but one that epitomized the attitude of men who would go down in history for their bravery and tenacity.

Internal strength is one of the characteristics most commonly mentioned by people when you ask them what makes a man. Former Green Bay Packers football coach Vince Lombardi (or General George S. Patton, depending on who you talk to) once said, "Fatigue makes cowards of us all." Isn't it easier to quit when we are tired or run-down? When life is ganging up on you, doesn't it seem easier to "slip" and look at pornography on the Internet or go out for a beer with the guys? Internal strength is what helps a man keep from quitting when things are tough. It's a "strength under control" that women and children can rely upon to always be there for them. This intestinal fortitude is what we must exhibit during times of struggle.

Duty is also often mentioned as an important character trait for authentic masculinity. Duty compels men to perform necessary acts for the benefit of others even when they would rather not. Duty is a moral obligation to act, despite our opinions. We do what has to be done whether we like it or not.

Loyalty and honor are also prized traits of a "man among men." Honor itself may be at the heart of masculinity. Honor, to my mind, is the single most important character trait for a man to possess, yet one that our culture seems to devalue more with each passing day.

But here are some character traits that we don't often associate with positive, healthy, authentic masculinity. Let's consider how these traits play a role in our development as men.

Action

Watch your thoughts, for they become words.
Watch your words, for they become actions.

Watch your actions, for they become habits.
Watch your habits, for they become character.
Watch your character, for it becomes your destiny.

Frank Outlaw[1]

Men, we have to stand up and fight. Fight for our women and children, and our country. We have to take action and stop being passive bystanders in life. The values that we know in our hearts are good and honorable are under constant attack. We stand by and watch as the soulless specter of a relativistic culture and the greed of huge corporations steal the soul of our land. This is a call to action.

Look what we have come to. Our public schools force our children to learn that homosexuality is a good and healthy lifestyle. Counselors are allowed to take our underage daughters to have an abortion without our even being notified, much less giving our consent. Judges who are appointed for life interpret the law to suit their own belief systems. The media encourages our children to have premarital sex early and often. Sexually transmitted diseases are rampant. Our kids are jaded and cynical, having lost their innocence too early in life by being exposed to the worst that life throws at them.

I'm sick to death of watching men allow their sons and daughters to grow up without a moral compass to guide them. Guys, it takes so little to make such a big difference in the world. Don't let anyone tell you or make you think that you are not valuable. You are so valuable that people die without your leadership. What you do or don't do affects many lives for hundreds of years. People you don't know and will never meet will be touched in some way by your very presence on earth. Your children suffer mightily by your absence or your indifference, but are blessed beyond compare by your presence and affection.

Compare some inner-city neighborhoods with up to a 75 percent fatherless rate versus neighborhoods where active fathers and good men are involved with their families. In the former we see crime, drugs, run-down buildings and homes, gangs, and men preying upon women and children. In the latter we see well-taken-care-of homes and lawns, nearly no crime, no gangs, no perverts preying upon women and children. A father's (a *man's*) very presence keeps crime and deterioration at bay.

A while back I noticed that a street sign in our neighborhood had been "tagged" by vandals. Later that day I went back to remove the spray paint from the sign. When I got there, my friend Tom, a neighbor down the street, was already there and had cleaned the sign off using his own time and money. I was really proud to know Tom at that moment. Tom's a good man and a good neighbor. That's what real men do—they are not passive but rather take active roles in keeping their homes and neighborhoods safe from destruction and decay. When actions like graffiti are allowed to remain, it incrementally leads to greater levels of crime. I have seen no more tagging in our neighborhood. I believe it is because the person who did it realizes there are real men in the area, and the risk of getting caught and its consequences are too great to make it worth the effort.

But men don't act in haste. Their actions are well thought out. They never lash out in anger. They don't make rash decisions based on emotion. They don't quit.

However, having said that, I'm convinced that authentic men, real men, healthy men, are men of action. They do not sit back passively and let life come at them. They don't continually *react* to what life throws at them; they are proactive—they have an action plan for how to deal with life and with different circumstances that come up. Certainly there will be circumstances and situations where life throws you a curveball, and you have to be resourceful enough to react, but for the most part men need to be prepared to act. Like the Boy Scout motto says, "Always Be Prepared!" There are good reasons for that motto. If you are not prepared in the wilderness, you can die. If you are not prepared to lead your family, they can die, be taken captive, or worse.

Courage

I wanted you to see what real courage is, instead of getting the idea that courage is a man with a gun in his hand. It's when you know you're licked before you begin, but you begin anyway and see it through no matter what.

Atticus Finch in *To Kill a Mockingbird*

Freedom isn't free, you know—it comes with a cost. Part of that cost is having the courage to do things that need to be done—even if they are unpopular or seem overwhelming.

It takes a lot of courage to be a husband and a father. It takes a lot of courage to be a man as well—at least it does to be a good man. There are forces out there that want to keep you silent and ineffective as a man. So what ways can we exhibit courage?

Do you speak the truth in love? As husbands and fathers we have to have the courage to make decisions and stick with them even when they are unpopular with our wives and children. Do you speak up when teenagers (or adults) are hurling profanities around in a restaurant, movie theater, or ball game? What about holding people accountable for their actions?

I walked out of the movie theater into the foyer one day, and a friend of mine was reprimanding a teenage boy for treating a young lady inappropriately inside the movie. He didn't know either of the teenagers but that didn't make any difference; his goal was to protect the virtue of the young woman. That took a lot of courage, especially as a group of people quickly surrounded them. As popular opinion started to sway against him, my voice of support stemmed the tide. One good man was beatable—two men were not.

I don't claim to be more courageous than the next guy. Like many men, I struggle with complacency and the reluctance to be confrontational, especially in personal relationships. It's so much easier to take the easy route, but we have to be courageous to protect and guide our families.

When my daughter Kelsey was about sixteen years old, she surreptitiously got involved with chat rooms on the Internet. My wife had previously installed software on our computer that allowed us to see what she was emailing to other people. My wife did not consider monitoring software a violation of our children's privacy. She saw it as fulfilling her duty as a parent to protect them. One day my wife came to me and said that Kelsey had met a man on the Internet and was planning on meeting him. We questioned her about this man, and she said he was twenty years old (which was too old to date her anyway) and that he was a "good" guy (interestingly, she never asked how we knew about this guy).

115

Since warning bells were clanging in our heads, we had a policeman friend of ours run a criminal background check on this guy using his name and phone number that he had given her to call him with. Imagine our surprise (not!) when we discovered this guy was really a twenty-eight-year-old man in another state with a criminal record. Our policeman friend told us that there was nothing they could do until he did something illegal. However, he suggested that most predators will run from girls that have a male protective presence in their lives because it is too much trouble to deal with.

Armed with that knowledge, I gave our new "friend" a call one day. He did not answer his phone but called my number back right away. He very aggressively demanded, "Who is this?"

I calmly replied, "I am Kelsey's father, the girl you have been communicating with online for the past month or so, and I understand you are planning on meeting her." There was a pregnant pause on the other end.

"I just want you to know that I have run a criminal background check on you and know your name and where you live. I'd like to know what your intentions are regarding my daughter."

After stammering for a minute, he said, "We are just friends."

I said, "Well, then I'd also like to know what business a twenty-eight-year-old man has being *friends* with a sixteen-year-old girl—who is still a minor, by the way. It doesn't seem like a very wise decision for a grown man to make."

I think you get the drift of our conversation. Frankly, I was surprised he didn't just hang up on me.

In conclusion, Kelsey and this guy continued to communicate online with each other for a while, but it was clear that this man was not as anxious to meet my daughter as he had been before. Today he is long gone.

Despite my initial inclinations, I was able to maintain my composure while talking with this guy, which I think stopped things from escalating. ("A gentle answer turns away wrath, but a harsh word stirs up anger," Proverbs 15:1.) I didn't even have to threaten to show up at his house with a baseball bat and a bunch of my buddies (many with daughters who had eagerly volunteered for the trip in advance).

I have to admit, though, it took some courage to make that phone call. I had to fight my inclination to be passive rather than force myself into action. But that courage protected my daughter from a potentially extremely dangerous situation.

Decisive

> Perversion and corruption masquerade as ambiguity. I don't trust ambiguity.
>
> John Wayne

The Duke was a decisive man. He knew what he thought and he wasn't afraid to say it. He didn't appear to like fence-straddlers or double-minded people.

And he was right about ambiguity. Men who are ambiguous in the way they face life have no real guidelines they live by—no honor code. They are uncertain about what is right and what is wrong. Being ambiguous does not mean you are tolerant or open-minded. It means you are afraid of having an opinion or a belief system. A man like this is swayed by popular opinion and the opinions of others.

James 1:7–8 speaks of the man who is "double-minded," not receiving wisdom from the Lord because he is unstable in all his ways. Being unstable in all ways means a person cannot be trusted. It means a man doesn't have enough faith to stand by his convictions.

Have you ever been around a man who couldn't or wouldn't make a decision? I once worked with a man who literally could not make a decision. He would sit around wringing his hands, changing his opinion to match whoever had most recently shared theirs. It would have been funny if it was not so pathetic. He was the boss of a company and he nearly ruined it, costing the jobs and livelihood of hundreds of people. People who count on you are depending on you to be decisive.

I don't think a man should be hardheaded or closed-minded, but a man should know what he believes in and make a firm decision when necessary. There are many times during the course of raising a family when you have to be decisive about certain issues or situations. If you allow yourself to wallow in indecision or be paralyzed for fear of being wrong, it can cause great harm. The solution? Ask God for wisdom and then you will be prepared to be decisive when it's needed.

Wisdom

If I have seen further, it is by standing on the shoulders of giants.

Sir Isaac Newton

When I became a Christian, one of the first things I asked for was wisdom. I figured if it was good enough for King Solomon, the wisest man in the history of the world, it was good enough for me. As my kids became teenagers, I continued to pray for wisdom—sometimes in desperation. Now I pray that God will give me wisdom as I write books and speak at workshops because of the responsibility that entails. I also pray for wisdom in the operation of our ministry because of the lives we touch.

Raising children, operating a business or ministry, building a marriage, or being any kind of a role model all carry big responsibilities and even bigger consequences. In order to successfully carry the burden of those responsibilities, I've found that wisdom is a good friend to have walking alongside you. I've also discovered that the only true place to acquire wisdom is from God: "If any of you lacks wisdom, let him ask of God, who gives to all liberally and without reproach, and it will be given to him" (James 1:5 NKJV). I think it's pretty awesome that God will give us wisdom if we just ask him in faith. And unlike most people, he won't even reproach us or make fun of us for our ignorance but will give wisdom to us abundantly.

I was pretty well-read and educated before becoming a Christian ten years ago, but it wasn't until I earnestly began praying for God's wisdom and consistently reading his Word that I began to feel like I had an inkling of wisdom. Oh, I don't pretend to be some wise man, but I am better prepared for most situations in life. And many of the trials and tribulations of life are a little easier to deal with now. Sometimes I even see them in advance and can avoid making decisions that lead to mistakes.

With the mustard seeds of wisdom came the confidence to try things that I would never have attempted before. Trying new things and learning from them gave me more wisdom and hence even greater confidence. With that newfound confidence I became a better father, a better husband, and probably a better man as well.

Integrity

Of all the properties which belong to honorable men, not one is so highly prized as that of character.

Henry Clay

By far, integrity is mentioned by both men and women as the defining mark of authentic masculinity. While honesty is part of having integrity, it goes even further. Integrity winds and weaves its way through all aspects of a man's life.

One of the most important things a man can learn is to make decisions based on principles and not emotions. I've observed that women often make decisions based on emotions or feelings, but a man shouldn't. Too often feelings can change on a whim. But principles are like a rock foundation to build our house upon. This requires a large amount of self-discipline on the part of a man. The decisions I've made using my feelings are the ones I have regretted the most.

The movie *Lonesome Dove* illustrates the contrast between men who do have integrity and men who do not. In the movie, former Texas Rangers Captains Woodrow F. Call and Augustus McCrae are men of principle and integrity. They do not compromise their principles and have clear boundaries of what constitutes good, manly behavior. They are hard men in a hard land but play by the rules and look out for those under their charge.

Contrast that against the behavior of their former comrade Jake Spoon. Spoon has good looks, charm, and success with the ladies, but inside he is still a little boy. Spoon is lazy and always seeks the easy way. He is also a gambler and a drinker. He is morally ambiguous and, because he lacks confidence as a man, is easily led astray by other men who use his insecurities against him. He is swayed by the opinions and manipulations of evil men. He falls in with bad men and ends up an accessory to murder, eventually getting hunted down and hanged by Call and McCrae.

Spoon wasn't necessarily a bad man, but he was easily influenced by bad men. He did not have the backbone and courage to stand up for what he knew to be right. He lacked moral fortitude and succumbed easily to the peer pressure of men who intimidated him. He eventually found himself paying the severe consequences for actions he didn't even commit. Jake Spoon was a coward. He lacked integrity and died because of it.

A man with integrity always assumes responsibility for his actions—he never blames others. He is constantly evaluating his circumstances and decisions to ensure he is acting in the best interests of others.

Leadership

In the movie *300* about the battle of Thermopylae, King Xerxes of Persia tells King Leonidas of the Spartans, "I would kill half my men for victory."

To which Leonidas replies, "And I would die for any *one* of mine."

That's servant-based leadership. Our cynical and complacent culture would say the willingness to die for someone else is foolish. But if your wife and children, friends and neighbors, co-workers and employees know that you would sacrifice your own needs for their benefit, it makes them more willing to follow your leadership. Your wife and children need to know that you would die for them. That's powerful! Tell your family, because they need to hear those words spoken—but then live it as well. Our actions speak louder than our words. We can tell our families that we would die for them, but if our actions show otherwise on a daily basis, what are they to believe?

Servant-based leadership requires selflessness. Selflessness is the opposite of selfishness in that it requires the willingness to sacrifice for the benefit of others. A man must be willing to sacrifice for his wife and children even if it means taking a hit to his pride.

A servant leader also needs compassion. He must be compassionate toward the needs and weaknesses of others. Jesus showed compassion to many who were sick or weak, and so we need to show compassion to those less fortunate than us.

Healthy leadership also requires the ability to know when to back off on an issue. A leader understands that he has to pick his battles. He knows when to draw a line in the sand and stand and fight, or when to compromise in the best interests of others.

I tell groups of parents that, especially with teenagers, you have to pick your battles. If you turn every issue into a battle, you will eventually lose the war. You need to determine your core values and draw a line in the sand around those issues. Some of the other things that are less consequential you need to let slide—if you don't, your teenager will eventually rebel against your leadership and authority.

Leadership in the face of adversity inspires a courage that bonds people together. Our actions through servant-based leadership unite and empower others in the face of overwhelming odds. It helps them to be everything God intended for them.

Perseverance

I love old sayings. They always have a lot of wisdom gained from real life. For instance, "It's always darkest just before dawn." Someone knew that from the experience of being out in the woods or being scared in the middle of the night. However, they also recognized that it applied to other, more metaphorical, situations as well. I heard Chuck Swindoll talking on the radio about the life of Charles Spurgeon. Mr. Spurgeon noted that every time his life got difficult and it seemed the darkest, that was just before God was ready to bless him and move him to a new place or stage in his life. It got darkest just before the light came. It caused me to realize that was true in my life and probably in most people's lives as well. It always does seem darkest and I get depressed and anxious and feel unworthy or incapable just before something breaks through and God blesses me. I think the lesson here is one of perseverance.

God blesses our perseverance in times of trouble, our faith even when things seem dark. Too many of us quit when life is at its most difficult—we quit when just a little more persistence would lead us into God's blessings. We quit just before God can bless us with his treasures. James 1:12 says, "Blessed is the man who perseveres under trial, because when he has stood the test, he will receive the crown of life that God has promised to those who love him."

Our first two years of operating the Better Dads ministry were so financially difficult. I certainly wasn't used to living by faith on God's daily provision. It was hard and I wanted to quit numerous times and get a job. Frankly, I was more than a little scared. But something about that verse stuck with me. I knew with all my heart God had chosen the path for my life that I was now walking. But it's one thing to know something in your heart, it's another to walk in the dark and have faith that God will not let you step off a cliff. I think perseverance is having faith under duress. That experience taught me a lot about faith and about trusting God. It matured me and grew me to where I needed to be to become dependable for the responsibilities God was going to entrust to me.

Life is full of disappointments. Throughout my whole life, people (starting with my parents) have been telling me I wasn't good enough to accomplish the things I wanted to do. I've had to overcome many challenges and roadblocks. People have said bad things about me that were not true and were very unfair. But I cannot allow that to stop me from being the best man I can be in my job, as a father and husband, or with my ministry. People count on me, and people count on you.

God uses hard times to perfect us. He often uses our suffering to correct and instruct us. However, it is important to remember that God is not always the author of our struggles—the evil one is eager to derail us at every opportunity. That is why it is important to ask God "Why?" whenever we find ourselves in a difficult circumstance. What is God trying to teach us? What do we need to learn from this struggle? My friend asked "Why?" when his son was born with Down syndrome. My daughter asked me why she was born with a cleft lip. Why did she have to suffer stares and taunting throughout her life? My friend asks why his wife has a mental illness.

I don't know the answer to those questions, but I do know that God empowers us through our struggles to be able to use the compassion and experience we learn in order to help others. God is near to those who are wounded in spirit.

Doing the right thing for the right reason and failing is not failure—it is faithfulness, and God always rewards faithfulness. If you do the best you can, and you do everything possible to succeed, then you have nothing to be ashamed of and should have no regrets. Don't be discouraged. The only true failure is not trying. Life will knock us down. Failure is not getting up again. We cannot control other people's actions or their decisions; we can control only our attitude and our response to them. Your example of perseverance in tough situations and how you respond to them could change someone's life—and you may never even know it.

A man—a real man—is one who gets knocked down and gets back up again and again no matter how tough or difficult the circumstances.

Patience

I don't suffer fools gladly. Patience is not one of my virtues—especially while driving. It's why I'm reluctant to put a Christian bumper sticker on my car. But I've learned that one of the most valuable traits in life is patience. God has worked hard over the course of my life trying to teach me this character trait. In fact, my wife thinks God put her in my life specifically to teach me that lesson.

While I believe it is important for men to be decisive, one thing I've learned over the years is to have patience, especially in the face of making tough decisions or solving difficult problems. Some men act rashly. My initial reaction to a situation is to make a quick decision to solve the problem so we can move on. But I've discovered that strategy is often flawed. In both business and relationships I've found that if I give the situation some time, especially if emotions are involved, then things seem to settle and often the situation works itself out. Concerns that seemed large at the moment become nonissues. Now I purposefully try to delay making a decision until the last possible moment. This allows me to think it through, it allows God to work in his timing, and it allows other factors to take place that might make the circumstance moot. I use this strategy for making purchases as well. If I want to buy something badly, I wait until at least twenty-four hours pass before making the purchase. Nearly always I find I did not want or need that item as much as I thought I did. This same approach is helpful with our children. While instant reinforcement is sometimes a good tactic, generally if I wait awhile before reacting to a situation involving one of my kids, I end up making a better decision.

The one regret many older men have is that they were not more patient when they were young husbands and fathers. They regret things that they said rashly in anger—things that cannot ever be taken back.

Our families need us to be steady and consistent as leaders. That requires being patient and not having unrealistic expectations of those under our guidance and leadership. People learn in many different ways, and this includes our children. One person learns best by hearing or reading, another learns best through watching, and yet another learns best by touching something or actually performing a task. And so I use a variety of techniques to help everyone learn the best way possible according to their bent. I will lecture with words, but also reinforce my points with movie video clips. I also introduce some object lessons where people can touch an object, and will use PowerPoint presentations and overheads to let people see written words. I also use stories as much as possible. People can relate them to their own experiences and thus reinforce the knowledge they've already gained.

My point is that it requires patience to help individuals learn through their specific learning style. If I want to be effective with both my family and others, I have to be willing to meet them at their level of need and not just what I think is best or which style suits me. If you want to be effective as a man, you must be patient enough to find where you can best help others and then meet them at their need.

Besides, it's a lot less stressful when we have patience instead of getting worked up over something we cannot control anyway—like traffic.

Conclusion

This is not an exhaustive list of all the character traits that men should strive to build and live their lives by. But hopefully they give us some food for thought on what a man should be like. Most men know in their hearts that they should strive to be honorable, to be loyal, and to have manly strength. Those are sometimes the easiest to recognize but often the most difficult to live out. However, some of the traits we reviewed above help make that transition from recognition to action that much easier.

8

The Lord of the Rings

It often seems as if the church is working in collusion with a culture bent on emasculating men and turning raw male material into pliable, defanged images of its own liking.

Rick Bundschuh,
Passed Thru Fire: A Call for a Christian Rite of Passage to Guide Boys into Godly Manhood

MEN LIVE UP to whatever expectations are placed upon them. Unfortunately, today's culture doesn't have very high expectations of men. If we are not to be doomed to living down to society's low expectations of us, then we must set high standards for ourselves.

I have found that testing myself against situations that are challenging and then coming out the other side has developed that core self-confidence I previously lacked. For instance, there is just something empowering to a man when he learns how to take care of himself in the wilderness. Learning how to start a fire, use a compass, hunt, fish, build a shelter, and stay alive even when lost is empowering. A guy who can survive and fend for himself in the wild has a fundamental confidence and calmness about him, because no matter what else happens, he knows he can survive off the land.

Frankly, I don't suffer halfheartedness well. If you can't do something with passion and dedication, then don't do it at all. Men develop passion when they are confident in their masculinity. Until then, they are using their energies to worry about their image and trying to prove their manhood.

This chapter describes the bridges between boyhood and manhood. A man's life consists of a journey from being a helpless child to moving into competent manhood, eventually passing into "elder statesman" status. It requires dealing with issues such as learning self-reliance skills as a boy, relational and self-sacrificing traits as a man, and the changing physical and emotional issues as an older man. These rites of passage are fraught with questions and fears that usually require the help of other men to circumnavigate. It's been my experience that most of us face the same struggles—we are never as unique as we fear or hope.

Men of Valor

Freedom is never more than one generation away from extinction. We didn't pass it to our children in the bloodstream. It must be fought for, protected, and handed on for them to do the same, or one day we will spend our sunset years telling our children and our children's children what it was once like in the United States where men were free.

President Ronald Reagan

"Men of valor"—that has a nice ring to it, doesn't it? *Valor* means strength of mind or spirit that enables a person to encounter danger with firmness; a personal bravery or heroic courage when facing danger. It's what I think men should personify.

Some occupations require us to show valor and bravery on a daily basis. Policemen and firemen are people who run toward danger when everyone else runs away from it. Soldiers face danger every day. Paramedics and EMTs rescue people who have been in terrible accidents. Doctors and nurses heal the sick and wounded. Hospice workers and special education teachers bless the lives of people that others are uncomfortable around.

Each of the people in these professions shows valor by their actions to bless the lives of those around them every day. It is a conscious choice they make, and most sacrifice mightily because of it.

So what does valor look like and why does it matter in a man's life? And how does it factor into authentic masculinity?

Boys and men need challenges. We thrive on them. When we lead safe, complacent, sedentary, passionless lives, we atrophy and slide into decay. Most men produce these challenges either by playing sports (or vicariously experience them through television) or testing themselves man against man or men against men. Sometimes we put ourselves in situations where we challenge nature (mountain climbing, space travel, or hunting), or even challenge ourselves against our peers (business, individual accomplishments, and so on). But there are greater ways to challenge ourselves as men.

Even though sports do not necessarily develop authentic masculinity, they do often bring out the best in men. If there is a man more deserving of honor in the world of sports than Jackie Robinson, I don't know who it would be. Mr. Robinson broke the color barrier in professional baseball. He was subjected to incredible stress and pressures as well as taunting, threats, and hate mail from fans and players alike. Yet he performed his craft with dignity and style. He was a fiery competitor yet controlled his temper so that he never sank to the level of his detractors. He was a man to be admired. He realized he was involved in something bigger than himself, bigger than his feelings, bigger than his wants or needs. He paved the way for countless men of all races and ethnicities to become part of "America's Favorite Pastime."

Like Jackie Robinson, Henry "Hammerin' Hank" Aaron also faced hatred and racism at its worst as he methodically approached and surpassed the all-time home run record held by Babe Ruth. Mr. Aaron always conducted himself with class and dignity despite the way he was treated by others. He let his actions speak louder than his words—something many of today's athletes do not seem to understand.

As long as we are talking about baseball players, I couldn't leave out Brooks Robinson, as he was my boyhood hero. I still have his baseball card on top of my dresser. It inspires me to continue on with consistency and steadfastness. Elected to the Hall of Fame in 1983, Brooks by his own admission lacked the physical skills to be a star athlete. Yet through dedication, hard work, and practice he will go down as the greatest third baseman ever to play the game of baseball, winning a

Golden Glove award for sixteen consecutive seasons, the World Series MVP in 1970, and the league's Most Valuable Player and All-Star Game MVP award in 1964. Nicknamed "The Human Vacuum Cleaner," his clutch performances in times of pressure made winners of him and his team. He inspires me as a man that even though I may not have been given the gift of greatness, I can still be great.

Sometimes even politics aids men on the journey to develop authentic masculinity (although more often it seems to squelch or pervert it). President Jimmy Carter was not my ideal model as a president, but no one can say that he has not used his influence and masculine power for the good of others. He spends a significant portion of his time working with Habitat for Humanity building homes for those who might otherwise never be able to obtain one. Additionally, Carter is one of the few men with the courage to publicly admit what most men are afraid to when he said, "I've looked on many women with lust. I've committed adultery in my heart many times. God knows I will do this and forgives me."

Lastly, while I am not foolish enough to think being in the military will "make a man out of you," and I don't look back on my stint with any special fondness, I do believe it has the potential to bring out the best in masculinity.

Are men made for violence? Maybe—perhaps that's why football and boxing are so popular with men, violent movies and videos games are bigger sellers, and hunting and fishing are the biggest hobbies of men.

I don't know if men are born violent or if our environment creates it within them. But I do know that violence is sometimes a necessary requirement to battle evil, and men are especially equipped to perform that task. Most often, men in the military have been called upon throughout history to perform that role.

Pacifists argue that our culture creates wars unnecessarily, and I understand their concerns. And some academics and scholars (typically of the soft sciences) have contended that the military serves only to pervert masculinity, turning men into what Sam Keen condescendingly refers to as "the Manchurian candidate," a hypnotized agent of the state waiting to be called into active service by the bugle call of "Duty," "Honor," "Patriotism."[1]

After having served in the military, I remember in college having a professor who was challenging the class by contemptuously saying that the US had a "John Wayne" mentality. While I don't always agree with our foreign policies, a heated debate ensued about whether military force is sometimes necessary. I contended that a bully will not stop being a bully no matter how much you cajole him. Sometimes he needs to be punched in the nose or he will never stop torturing other people. When evil men torture and kill innocent people, it is a good man's responsibility to intercede. On a takeoff of Edmund Burke's quote, Martin Luther King Jr. once said, "Evil prospers when good men do nothing." Sometimes we have to go toe to toe, bare knuckles with evil. Unfortunately, the sap-draining ethos of apathy and passivity (and frankly, selfishness) that pervades our culture wishes all bad things would just go away without any effort on our part.

But I contend that, for all the faults of the military (and horrors of war), it also develops many aspects of a man's character that he needs to become authentically masculine. (If you want the hair on your neck to stand up, just go to www.medalofhonor.com and read about all of the Medal of Honor winners and their valiant, heroic deeds.) We see many young men—aimless and unfocused, perhaps even in trouble—that a stint in the military has straightened out, teaching them self-discipline and self-control. The military is also a necessity to prepare men to fight evil and injustice, and to protect our freedoms.

Every soldier, sailor, marine, or airman who has fought or died in a war is a hero. Say what you want about war and the military. Many of the popular books written about masculinity by social scientists decry the military and what they represent. However, without the men who have served gloriously in the military, none of us would have the freedom to complain and criticize these institutions.

Authentic masculinity protects women and children from evil and from harm. Evil men kill innocence. Evil men use women and children for personal gain and self-gratification. Evil men operate the sex industries, the drug trade, slavery trafficking, and every other ill perpetrated upon the human race. Evil men must be stopped by good men. Good men who do step up and stop evil should be celebrated and honored.

So to all the leathernecks, dogears, deck apes and snipes, grunts, and flyboys out there, past and present, I salute you. You are men of valor and deserve our respect and honor. Don't ever let anyone tell you that your contribution was insignificant or wrong—it meant something and so do you.

A Dysfunctional Rite of Passage

Having grown up in an emotionally violent and often physically dangerous home, I have the distrust of, fear of, and contempt for drinkers that only the child of an alcoholic can understand and appreciate. As I grew up, I was determined to control my own safety and well-being. Because I had been a victim as a child, I judged myself harshly for not being able to defend myself against the adults in my life. (It doesn't make sense, but many victims feel this way.) Consequently, when I left home and joined the military, I began a process to make myself invincible—to protect myself. Having wrestled all through high school, I began boxing and learning self-defense techniques in the service. I went out of my way to prove my courage to myself and others by engaging in brawls throughout the Mediterranean and other ports of call. I was determined never to be a victim again. Yet my very actions victimized me in a variety of ways.

I soon recognized the folly of this behavior and just wanted to be left alone. I developed a "tough guy" persona. While I was in the Navy, I got a tattoo on each of my forearms. This was back in the mid-1970s when only sailors, bikers, and ex-convicts sported tattoos. These tattoos were a symbol of my manliness, or at least my toughness, designed to keep people away from me in bars and other seedy venues. It worked. No one bothered me . . . except to pick a fight to prove how tough and manly they were. The only people this façade kept away were healthy people who could have loved me and helped me grow.

After mustering out of the military and bouncing around awhile, I used a variety of extreme sports such as rock climbing and skydiving to prove my courage and manhood. Eventually I started my own business to make a lot of money and prove my manhood. But on the golf course with corporate executives, I felt massively out of place with my tattoos, looking as if I had just been released from prison. I soon had the tattoos removed through a series of laser treatments, which hurt more (and were a heck of a lot more expensive) than getting the original tattoos did. The laser beam shoots out pulses of light that "spatter" the dye pigment molecules, allowing your body to absorb the ink. Imagine having a rubber band snapped really hard on your skin thousands of times over and over again.

My personally designed rite of passage to manhood was characterized by challenging myself to climb over the backs of other males in order to prove my manhood. But it was a fruitless and frustrating experience. And afterward, I still did not know if I was a man or not. If you think you have to prove yourself a man, you're probably not.

Many men I've spoken with did not know when they first "became a man"; in fact, some still do not know if they are a man at all. Young men, particularly gang members, use all sorts of bizarre and dangerous rituals to prove themselves. Even many older men are still unsure of themselves and use accomplishments, performance, rituals, or even abuse to attempt to show the world their manliness.

Our culture typically does not provide boys with a model to recognize and achieve their manhood through ceremonies or passages. Other cultures now and in the past used a variety of typically difficult and painful challenges to let a boy know he has entered into manhood. Our lack of some kind of rite of passage today keeps young men from knowing when they are accepted into the company of men and leaves them continually trying to prove their manhood to themselves and others, often in dangerous and destructive ways.

Rituals and Initiations

Many cultures have a ceremony or ritual that marks the passage from boyhood to manhood. Perhaps the most recognizable in the US is the Jewish ceremony of Bar Mitzvah. Bar Mitzvah literally translated means "son of obligation," when a young man becomes fully responsible to observe the commandments of the Torah (first five books of the Old Testament). A Jewish boy automatically becomes Bar Mitzvah on his thirteenth birthday. The ceremony to mark his arrival at manhood has several customs, including a celebration ceremony. During the Sabbath on or after his thirteenth birthday, a boy recites the blessings for the Torah reading, reads the week's portion from the Torah and Haftara (selections from the books of the Prophets), and/or gives a discussion of that week's Torah portion. He may also lead part or all of the morning prayer services. Once Bar Mitzvah has occurred, the boy is now personally responsible for his actions.

Other cultures also put young men through rituals and ceremonies in order to mark their passage into manhood. Several tribes in Papau New Guinea use initiation ceremonies to mark the passage of boys to men. One of the more gruesome and bloody is performed by the *Iatmul* tribe. The teenage boys who choose to go through the ceremony are separated from their mothers and other women. They must first run a gauntlet of beatings with whips and sharpened sticks in order to enter the men's compound. Once there they are subjected to several days of humiliating ordeals and hazing ceremonies in order to humble them in preparation to become a man. The initiation ceremony consists of slicing each boy with deep razor blade cuts up to a thousand times. The cuts are rubbed with a mixture of clay and ash to make the scars rise, giving the appearance of "crocodile skin." This painful and bloody mutilation is performed without any anesthetic. Upon completion of this ordeal, the boys are considered men with all the rights and privileges that entails.

Boys of the *Maasai* tribe in Africa historically had to kill a lion with just their spear in order to become a warrior. Now, however, circumcision seems to be the main rite of passage (see Zulu ceremony below).

A *Comanche* boy was highly respected because he could become a warrior and die young in battle. As he approached manhood, a boy went on his first buffalo hunt. If he made a kill, his father honored him with a feast. Only after he had proven himself on a buffalo hunt was a young man allowed to go on a warpath.

When he was ready to become a warrior, at about age fifteen or sixteen, a young man first "made his medicine" by going on a vision quest (a rite of passage). Following this quest, his father gave the young man a good horse to ride into battle and another mount for the trail. If he had proved himself as a warrior, a Give Away Dance might be held in his honor. As drummers faced east, he and other young men danced. His parents, along with his other relatives and the people in the band, threw presents at his feet—especially blankets and horses symbolized by sticks.

Vikings were Scandinavian seafaring traders, warriors, and pirates who raided and colonized wide areas of Europe from the eighth to the eleventh century and reached east to Russia and Constantinople. Young Viking boys went on a vision quest before becoming men. The vision quest experience could be from one to four days and involved fasting while in the wilderness. The ritual used by the ancient Vikings was comparable to the Sioux and Comanche tribes' vision quest.

Spartan boys of ancient Greece were taken from their mothers at seven years of age and placed in a "boot camp" program designed to turn them into warriors and men. They attended a military school that was increasingly more difficult until the age of eighteen. This program included vigorous training and painful trials that were required to be endured. The boys were not fed well and were told that it was fine to steal food as long as they did not get caught. If they were caught, they were beaten. The boys marched without shoes to make them strong. It was a brutal training period. They walked barefoot, slept on hard beds, and worked at gymnastics and other physical activities such as running, jumping, javelin and discus throwing, swimming, and hunting. As they were lightly clothed and had no bedding to speak of, children would often put thistles in their pallets because the prickling sensation made them feel warmer. They were subjected to strict discipline and harsh physical punishment; indeed, they were taught to take pride in the amount of pain they could endure.

At eighteen, Spartan boys became military cadets and learned the arts of war. At that age they would have to go through what was known as the gauntlet. They would have to run around a group of older children, who would flog them continually with whips, sometimes to death. On leaving the training academy they would be sorted into groups, whereupon some were sent into the countryside with nothing and forced to survive on their skills and cunning; this was called the *krypteia*, believed to be an initiation rite to seek out and kill helots (serfs) who were considered to be troublesome to the state, or those who were found to be wandering the countryside with no good reason.

At twenty years of age, they joined the state militia—a standing reserve force available for duty in time of emergency—in which they served until they were thirty years old, although they remained in the active reserves until age sixty.

In the *Zulu* tribe of South Africa, young boys go through a stage of initiation when they enter adulthood. Boys start their initiation at the age of around sixteen to eighteen. The male initiation process includes circumcision (ouch!), seclusion (especially from females), humiliation, and being taught discipline and respect for their culture. The boys are taken into an isolated area and stay in grass huts. They wear only one small piece of clothing around the waist before circumcision. No one is allowed to see them, with the exception of the older women relatives who give the boys food and watch out for them. After the process of being circumcised, the boys are said to be "cleaned." They are given new clothes (mainly animal hide made by the older women) to show that they have a fresh, new look. After that they go back to their tribe, and are now seen as men and accepted by the members of the tribe. The clothing they wear shows how confident they are to be men.

What Men Wish They Knew

Speaking to and working with men over the years has given me several interesting insights into some of the regrets men have or the issues that they wish someone had shared with them on the road to manhood.

Many wished they would have had some preparation for or even initiation into the responsibilities of manhood. Most men shared the fear they encountered when suddenly faced with the responsibility of marriage and the birth of a child. One man told me that over the years he has practically begged his dad for advice as various circumstances arose, like buying a home. His dad would never answer any of his questions. It wasn't that he would have blindly followed his dad's advice; it was just that he craved input from someone who had already walked the path.

Many men regret decisions they made regarding their family when they were young. Some spent too much time at work instead of developing stronger relationships at home. Just today a man told me his son had died at the age of twenty-four and how much he looks back with regret at all the time he spent at work instead of with his boy.

Some were too passive or afraid to address an issue that needed to be resolved—like problems with their marriage. Rather than confront it, they let it go. Now it is too late. Others had children out of wedlock or divorced their wives. To a man, they regret not working harder to keep those relationships alive. Still others, usually older men, wish they had shown more physical affection to their children.

Many men shared that they were completely unprepared for understanding women. They had received no training or advice on dealing with the strange emotions and sometimes bizarre rituals of the opposite sex. Many of the needs of a woman caught them completely off guard. Additionally, they entered relationships with unrealistic expectations of their wives. They also wished someone had explained their sexuality to them from a man's perspective. Many of their fathers dealt with that issue just like their fathers before had—they ignored it.

Men also said that they wish they would have understood that others don't always perceive life as they do. Older men wish they had not been so judgmental about people who were different than they were. They now recognize that everyone has something to offer, and if you are not aware of that, you might miss it. They know that they must have realistic expectations of others.

One seventy-five-year-old man I spoke with was a wealth of knowledge. He has been both married and a pastor for the last fifty-three years of his life. As he nears the end of a well-lived life, he was able to reflect upon several things he wished he had known as a younger man. He shared with me what he described as the "biggest breakthrough" of his life:

REAL MEN

- Real men try to treat everybody decently.
- Real men don't hit women or children. Ever.
- Real men don't feel the need to strut and swagger.
- Real men don't try to prove their masculinity.
- Real men know that bullies are people who want to be men but aren't.
- Real men judge people by how they treat other people.

I raised three boys and a little girl. When they were young, I was very strict with them because I wanted them to turn out good. The one regret I have in life though is not that I was strict with them—I still would be strict—but I wish I had blended that strictness with more love and affection. I wish I had been quicker to forgive and slower to punish. God really rammed this home to me one day when I was preparing for a sermon. As I read through Scripture, God spoke to me and said, "I don't punish my children." I thought this cannot be right—surely God does punish His children. But as I looked through the Bible, it became clear to me that God does not punish us—His children. He chastises us, corrects us, and even disciplines us when we are wrong, but he never punishes in anger. He loves us too much. The image I had was of a crooked branch growing in the wrong direction. To correct or discipline it is to gently help it straighten out. To punish it would be to break it off. I never looked at punishing my kids again in the same light.

I wish an older man would have shared advice like that with me when I was a young man.

What Men Fear

Over the years many men have shared their fears with me. The following are fears that most men seem to share in common. They might not always be spoken of, but they linger within the hidden consciousness of a man.

One very honest man told me, "I have many fears that rule my life. I have a fear of failure and a fear of change or the unknown. It causes me to be excessively critical and pessimistic when faced with new challenges as a way to avoid them. It is debilitating and paralyzing when I allow this fear to dominate me."

Men fear being inadequate. It's not the same as failing. When we fail, we just get back up (hopefully), but being inadequate is humiliating. It means we cannot "cut the mustard" as a man. Men who act overly macho—who push people around—are that way because they are afraid of being inadequate. They are always weak, insecure, and scared. They try to compensate for that by making others afraid. That way everyone else is just like them—afraid.

Men raised without fathers often experience apprehension about becoming fathers themselves because they never had that role modeled for them. They also do not understand how a man is supposed to treat a woman because that was never modeled for them as well.

Men fear being dominated. It smacks of not only being inadequate but also being powerless to do anything about it. To be dominated is to be humiliated as a man. Men know that losing is sometimes inevitable, but being dominated is unbearable. It's one of the reasons pro football has rules against "taunting" an opponent.

Not being masculine enough is another big fear men have—not being masculine enough means not being considered a man. Most guys would rather suffer through any physical pain than not be considered a man. That's why being disrespected by his wife is so painful. When the one person who knows him best treats him with disrespect, it is like saying to the world that he is not man enough.

Loss of significance is a big fear for men. Demotion or the loss of a job, being ridiculed, or even having a baby usurp your place of importance at home are demoralizing and frightening to men.

Rejection is also very difficult for most men. I'm certainly afraid of rejection—I hold my breath every time I send a chapter in to my editor. Rejection keeps us from attempting greatness. But even on a smaller scale the sting of rejection bites deep. Not getting a promotion we deserve, asking and being turned down by our wives for sex, even being ignored in a grocery store line are subtle stabs to our manhood. And it only gets worse as we get older.

As men get older, we start experiencing changes—ones we don't always like, ones that make us afraid. After a certain age our bodies start deteriorating, and we can't physically perform the things we could when we were younger. I know at my age I cannot do most of the things I used to be able to on the basketball court. My mind still functions well—better than it used to, in fact. But my body either refuses to do what my mind tells it or it takes at least a second or two longer to execute.

In addition our sex drive starts diminishing (a little anyway). And even if the mind is willing, sometimes the flesh is weak. We start having health issues that show us we are not invincible anymore. We become invisible to young women. We also become softer emotionally—our hearts soften as we age.

Not only do we experience these physiological and emotional changes, but often a man wakes up one day and realizes he wasted his life on achievements that are inconsequential. He has accomplished nothing of lasting significance. He recognizes that he won't be remembered for anything of consequence. He spent his most productive years striving for monetary success that has become dust in the wind.

We don't like all these changes and so they can be frightening and a bit overwhelming. And so in our fear and panic over our loss of immortality we look to relive our youth—a do-over, if you will—another chance to live our lives and do a better job. We experience what is often called a "midlife crisis." And so in this crisis men buy the toys (fast cars, clothes, jewelry) of their youth and try their best to see if they are still attractive to young women (do I still have "it"?).

At the very least this is an attempt to delay the onset of their decline in many men's minds—to prove we are still immortal. This is probably not a conscious thought process for most men, but one that many seem helpless to follow nonetheless.

Lastly, some of the biggest challenges men report center around being a husband and a father. Most men struggle with being unselfish and serving others—I know I do. Many of us guys seem to have a selfish nature, and trying to overcome those natural inclinations is a constant struggle. But it is more worthy to give than to receive. There is a certain nobility about men who are able to conquer this bent and give their life in service of others.

Conclusion

The journey to manhood is difficult and confusing, especially if not guided by an older male or males. The biggest challenge males face in our culture today is the lack of intentional mentoring by older men throughout our lives. Additionally, we have no initiation or ceremony to let a boy know he has graduated and joined the legions of manhood. Combine that with a lack of defined roles and character traits that a man should live his life according to and we have a recipe for disaster. We are seeing the consequences of our shortsightedness in allowing young males to grow up without a community of men to guide them. Other men, those raised by healthy mentors, just know how to be a man without even thinking about it.

Manhood and authentic masculinity are a journey, not a destination. It is a lifelong process of growth and adjustment. The journey can be frustrating and frightening or it can be exhilarating and exciting. You'll take that journey whether you want to or not. Understanding your strengths and weaknesses now can make that journey much more fun and productive. And when that journey is fun, we walk this earth with our heads held high and a bounce in our step—because we are men, and being a man is good.

9

The Dirty (Half) Dozen

Quicksand and Other Traps

I had no sensation of sliding [down the slippery slope of deception]. But of course we never notice the descent until we're rocketing along at high velocity.

Dean Koontz, Odd Thomas speaking
to Brother Knuckles in *Brother Odd*

ATECHNIQUE THE ESKIMO use for hunting wolves is to coat the blade of a knife with blood and let it freeze. This process is repeated several times until the blade of the knife is completely coated and appears harmless. The knife is then secured in the ground, ice, or some other stable place with the blade exposed. When the wolf finds the knife, he will begin licking the exposed blade with increasing passion as he tastes the thawing blood. However, as he gets more and more excited, the wolf doesn't realize that the blade of the knife is slicing his tongue and that it is his own blood that he now tastes. Eventually, the wolf will bleed to death by his own doing.

The same thing can happen in our lives with addictions such as alcohol, drugs, sex, pornographic materials, gambling, or any other enticement that sucks us down into the depths of darkness. It begins slowly, perhaps with an occasional drink or visit to an inappropriate website. At the time, it seems okay, and we don't believe that we could become a victim. "There is a way that seems right to a man, but in the end it leads to death" (Prov. 14:12).

I loved watching adventure movies as I was growing up, and one of the things that fascinated me was quicksand. It was always waiting in the path of the hero to suck him into its suffocating grasp. And it was invisible even when it was right in front of him. The interesting thing about quicksand was that you could never get out of it by yourself. You had to have the help of a partner. The other thing about it was that the harder you struggled, the deeper and faster you sank.

Like quicksand, the following traps wait to ensnare us if we are not alert and vigilant to guard ourselves against them. And like quicksand, most of these take other men to help us get out and stay out of these sinkholes of life.

Passivity

For the ordinary man is passive. Within a narrow circle (home life, and perhaps the trade unions or local politics) he feels himself master of his fate, but against major events he is as helpless as against the elements. So far from endeavoring to influence the future, he simply lies down and lets things happen to him.

George Orwell, "Inside the Whale"

Passivity is one of the "two big curses" of masculinity—apathy being the other. So many men fall into the trap of passivity in their lives and then resent the mundane and insignificant lives they lead, often causing them to lash out at their loved ones. There is an epidemic of passive men in our culture today. Many of these men have been raised with no positive male influences in their lives, only female role models. These men refuse to lead and make decisions in relationships. They are content to let the women in their lives make all the decisions and take care of them. Some guys might think that sounds like a good deal. But it is emasculating for the man and horribly frustrating for his woman.

Unfortunately, for a variety of reasons the church often encourages passivity in men. One non-Christian man told me, "Whenever I have been to church, I always meet a lot of nice guys. But they strike me as being very passive, like they would never defend a woman if they had to. They are not the kind of men who I want to be around."

Passivity is unhealthy because it allows life's circumstances to push us around, discouraging us from proactively tackling the events and challenges we are faced with. Passivity keeps us sitting on the couch instead of looking for healthy adventure in our lives. Then, because we are dissatisfied with our lives, we step into quicksand. As an example, most men fall into extramarital affairs not for sex but the craving for adventure and passion in their lives. Passivity not only keeps us from living lives of significance, but it stops us from using our masculine influence and power to lift others up to lead healthy, fulfilling lives.

Men who are passive just let life happen to them. They never take a stand—they are too pliable. They don't stay the course. They believe (or have been trained) that pride and aggression are somehow bad or wrong. But in our efforts to stem abuse of these masculine characteristics, the pendulum has swung too far in the opposite direction. It is vital that men understand that there is healthy pride and healthy aggression.

I am proud I was able to start and operate a successful small business for sixteen years. I am also proud of the fact that I have written and published a number of books. They are both accomplishments not too many people can say they have done. I do understand that God gets the ultimate credit, but I had to put forth the effort and make myself available to him in order for them to happen. So, I feel good about it. Also, if I had not been somewhat aggressive (in a healthy way), our fathering skills ministry would never have gotten off the ground and prospered. Again God gets the credit, but my wife would come home from work many days and say that she couldn't believe how many things I had made happen that day through sheer determination.

What happens when men are passive? Perhaps no organization in the history of our land has dedicated itself to raising the standard of producing men of honor and integrity more than the Boy Scouts of America. And yet they are under a vicious attack on all sides today, merely because an organization that puts men together with teenage boys to teach and train them to become healthy, authentically masculine males refuses to allow homosexual men to infiltrate its leadership ranks. Allowing that would be tantamount to allowing heterosexual men to spend unsupervised overnight campouts with groups of teenage girls. No one in their right mind would suggest that is a good idea.

And yet, how many men, while this great organization is under heavy, constant legal and media bombardment, have ventured so much as a verbal message of support? How many of us have provided financial aid while the BSA's funding has been drastically cut by organizations such as the United Way that choose to bend under politically correct special interest groups? How many of us have called and complained to our school districts when they have refused to allow the BSA to hold troop meetings in their facilities any longer? (Speaking of schools, did you know that as a man your voice carries a lot of weight with the schools? They typically only hear from mothers, so when a father speaks up it tends to have gravitas.) How many have taken the time to pick up the phone and call our local, state, or federal politicians to complain? How many of us have even sent a letter or made a phone call to BSA offering a message of support? How many of us have volunteered our time to help raise boys to become healthy men?

When men stand on the sidelines, with hands in pockets and faces downcast in shame—as Adam once did—all good things die. And once gone they are almost always gone forever.

Apathy

> There has got abroad a notion, somehow, that if you become a
> Christian you must sink your manliness and turn milksop.
>
> C. H. Spurgeon

The second big obstacle to authentic masculinity is apathy.
Apathy keeps men from fulfilling their destinies and walking
the path that God had planned for their lives. When we do
not walk the path that God intended for us, we live lives of
frustration, boredom, and irrelevance. Most of us are content
to lead comfortable, "normal" lives. But walking the path of
significance requires us to shrug off our apathy and become
energized with passion.

I owned an environmental engineering firm for sixteen years.
I distinctly remember the frustration of gradually recognizing
that no matter how hard or smart I worked, or how many hours
I put in, it seemed as if there was a giant glass ceiling that limited
the success of my business. It felt as though I was continually
banging my head against that ceiling in vain as I tried to push
and grow my business to the next level. In hindsight I now
understand that it was because that was *my* plan for my life
and not the Lord's. I could have succumbed to my inclination
to become apathetic and settle for my "lot in life." But I chose
instead to search for God's meaning for my life.

Today I know beyond a shadow of a doubt that I am fulfilling
God's mission for my life. I draw a great amount of satisfaction,
comfort, and gratification from that. Even though it is often difficult and the spiritual battle intense, I believe I am now living a
life of significance. I spend my efforts and masculine influence
to help others; to lift them up; to give them hope, encouragement, and honor. The other aspect of this is that once I started

walking the path of God's design, he began throwing open doors for me. Opportunities, connections, and improbable meetings with people of influence continually occur now. Situations and opportunities that could never have happened in my old business are nearly a commonplace occurrence with our ministry now. We see all these miraculous threads being weaved by God from various sources around the country. But we can't always see the tapestry that God is weaving. It is almost as if we are standing behind the tapestry as it is being weaved one thread at a time. Somewhere in the future we may be blessed to stand in front of the tapestry and see God's glorious creation.

I am excited and energized to get out of bed every day. Life is an adventure with all the danger, thrills, and joys that adventures contain. It is the most exciting, refreshing, and satisfying way to live I've ever experienced or ever hoped to.

God wants your life to be like that—he wants you to live a life of abundance. "I have come that they may have life, and that they may have it more abundantly" (John 10:10 NKJV). *Abundant* here means not only eternal life through salvation but *quality* of life. Through Christ, our life here on earth can reach a much higher quality, filled with nourishment, healing, and significance.

Had I allowed my natural inclination toward apathy to stop me from stepping out in faith, God would never have been able to use me in the incredible ways he does today. And I would have missed out on living a life beyond what I always dreamed.

Fear

If men as individuals surrender to the call of their elementary instincts, avoiding pain and seeking satisfaction only for their own selves, the result for them all taken together must be a state of insecurity, of fear, and of promiscuous misery.

Albert Einstein, *Out of My Later Years*

The biggest fear of most men is rejection. I used to think the biggest fear was fear of failure, but I think the fear of rejection is even more pronounced in most men. It's not always an obvious characteristic in men. This fear of rejection keeps men from attempting many things in life that would bless them and others. It's easier to sit on the sidelines than it is to risk being rejected. So we don't open ourselves up emotionally to our wives and children, we don't reach out to make friends, we don't strive for that promotion at work, we don't attempt greatness for fear of being rejected or ridiculed. Fear of rejection keeps us huddled under a blanket with a flashlight so the monsters don't get us.

I know a man who turns *everything* into a competition. It doesn't matter what it is—bike riding, hiking, hunting, even driving a car—he has a fierce compulsion to "win" at each of them. And if he loses, he is not very good company. I like friendly competition as much as the next guy, but making a win-at-all-costs situation out of every circumstance is pretty unhealthy. Unfortunately he has forced this value system upon his son who appears to resent it as he gets older, causing him to drop out of sports and anything that might contain a hint of competition. Now his wife has left him for another man because of his oppressive, overbearing nature.

The reason this man turns everything into a competition is not because he is fiercely competitive. It is because he is afraid. He is afraid of not matching up, of not being "man" enough, and so he needs the continual affirmation that he gets from competing and winning at trivial things that do not really matter in life. Like many men with this compulsion, he was not raised with a positive male role model as a guide. Hence, he is insecure and feels compelled to challenge other men to affirm his manliness.

One tendency of all men is to have their manliness validated by others through performance. Through competition in sports, the workplace, and accomplishments, we compare and compete with other men. If we match up favorably, we must be a man. If not, we are somehow less a man. If we perform well enough, we make more money, have more power, and attract more beautiful women. This need to measure ourselves against other men is a self-defeating process. It's not about being better than the guy next door, or having a bigger house than your neighbor, or having a better-looking wife than your friends, or being a better bowler than your buddies; it's about being a better man. And being a better man means shedding our fear of rejection, failure, and humiliation, and focusing our energies and passions on making the world a better place for everyone.

Fear clings to a man like stink on a monkey. Fear causes men to be socially and emotionally impotent. Fear of judgment keeps men from attempting to reach their dreams. Fear of failure stops them from living lives of honor, duty, and consequence.

It wasn't too long ago that a father was required to face danger from marauding bandits, wild animals, or warring tribes in order to physically protect his family. It's no wonder we men crave adventure and excitement. However, that kind of action required men to overcome and control their fear on a daily basis. Your family still needs that kind of protection from you—maybe not physically so much anymore, but certainly emotionally and psychologically. They need you to be just as brave as our forefathers. Unfortunately facing physical fear is sometimes easier for men than facing emotional or relationship-based fears. That's when we have to step up to the plate and risk failure and rejection the most. It's when we are willing to risk that we find the most blessings in the situation.

Fear is a lonely companion—I know. It is an exhausting and ultimately unfulfilling way to live. It is mere existence and survival, not an enriching, satisfying life.

Niceness

> Valorous niceness is often cowardly passivity in disguise.
>
> Paul Coughlin, *No More Christian Nice Guy*

A lot of men, especially Christian men, in our culture are nice guys. But it is often a niceness that disguises fear, passivity, apathy, and cowardice. Men are trained to be nice because it is unacceptable in most arenas of our culture for a man to be a man—to exhibit healthy masculinity. Particularly if he is assertive, passionate, and bold, he is feared by many segments of our culture.

Now understand there is nothing wrong with a man being nice. I try to be nice and extend kindness to all I meet. And most of the great men I know are very nice people—nice, but not soft. But if a man has been indoctrinated by his family, our culture, or even the church to *only* be nice, to never be assertive or even angry about anything, it can be devastating to his masculinity. These men assume a false humility and allow themselves to become doormats. They then internalize the anger created by feeling disrespected and either become passive-aggressive or irritated and angry in their actions with others. Unfortunately this kind of behavior is very destructive to a man's family. These men feel they are somehow defective and unworthy of respect—that their needs and wants are less important than other people's. Of course this brokenness wounds and emasculates them on a daily basis.

This type of belief steals a man's passion, energy, and courage. These guys are taught that passion, boldness, and intensity are wrong. So to keep up appearances they "stuff" any desire for those masculine character traits and end up being paralyzed and indifferent. They avoid confrontation and conflict at all cost, even shirking standing up to injustice.

I confess I don't relish conflict, especially with my wife. I'd rather avoid it if at all possible. But if that mentality spills over into all areas of our lives, we become unhealthy and ineffective as men. Healthy masculinity does not hide behind the false veneer of "niceness." Sometimes as men, fathers, and husbands, we must make decisions that make people mad or disappoint them. We cannot allow our desire to avoid conflict and be known as nice keep us from being effective in our responsibility as leaders.[1]

Weakness

A weak man has doubts before a decision; a strong man has them afterwards.

Karl Kraus, *Half-Truths and One-and-a-Half Truths*

Sometimes I see men who cry easily and often. Frankly, I'm always a little embarrassed. It's not that a man shouldn't cry; in fact, there are times when it's very appropriate for a man to cry. Too many men who deny and stuff their emotions suffer because of it. But a guy who doesn't have the inner strength to control his emotions, especially in inappropriate situations, might not be dependable enough to rely on during tough times.

I remember being at a wedding where the groom cried the whole ceremony to the point where he couldn't even recite his vows. I couldn't figure out if he was happy or miserable. I just knew I was embarrassed for him and didn't want to be like him.

A man's strength is what people rely on to lead and guide them when circumstances are hard or dangerous. In times of crisis I don't want to follow a sensitive man who cries easily; I want to follow a wise man of bold action and decision. Life is hard and full of crises. Those who follow and look up to you deserve a man under whose leadership they can feel safe and comfortable—one whose emotions are under control.

A real man does cry. I've cried at funerals of loved ones and when each of my children was born. I cry when I see the pain and suffering of innocent victims. Frankly, as I've gotten older I even leak a tear or two over movies more frequently than I'd like to admit. I watched a video on a website the other day of an actual abortion being performed. Anyone, man or woman, who can watch something like that and not weep doesn't have a heart. But in most situations a man's tears probably have a proper time and place.

Yes, I know that is probably an unpopular stance in today's emotional climate (don't get me started on the whole movement to feminize males). But I don't think men who cry are weak. A real man *is* tender, kind, compassionate, and loving.

The man who quits when things get difficult is weak. The man who takes off when raising a family becomes overwhelming is weak. The man who runs off with another woman when his marriage is struggling is weak. The man who quits his job with nothing lined up to replace it when he has a family to feed is weak. The man who lies, cheats, or steals because it is easier than hard work is weak. The man who picks on others' weaknesses to lift himself up is weak. The man who preys on those he is supposed to defend is weak.

Many young men today are soft and internally weak, especially those raised with only female influences. Frequently these young men are passive and indecisive. Some of these young men might appear vigorous and venture beyond the passivity that has been bred and instilled into them. Often, though, these young men get stuck in the adventure phase of masculinity. They rock climb, paddle hair-raising white water, and do all sorts of extreme sports. Girls are often attracted to these types of young men. They seem rugged, adventurous, passionate—all good qualities in a man. But unfortunately, these young men never grow beyond their need for self-gratification, they never evolve to the next stage of masculinity, that of sacrifice. Strength is the ability to put aside your own needs for the sake of another's. Weakness is placing your needs above everyone else's.

The smothering, overbearing presence of our post-post-modernist culture and its twisted sisters, radical feminism, political correctness, and relativism has gelded men. I was recently at a meeting brainstorming about how best to reach and then inspire uninvolved men to be better fathers. One of the men came up with a very good idea that was an "in your face" challenge to men. The women present immediately and vigorously vetoed the idea as being "too mean—we might offend someone." But men *need* to be challenged! Part of the reason so many men are passive, timid, milquetoast representatives of masculinity is that our culture and the church have been feminized to the point where they don't encourage or won't allow men to be men. Men are not challenged to greatness; they are not encouraged to change the world. I believe that a big part of why so many men bury themselves in drugs, alcohol, pornography, television, work, and other conscience-numbing activities is to deaden the pain they subconsciously feel by not being able to express their masculine soul. Men need challenges; they need risk.

Sir Ernest Henry Shackleton is reported to have placed what has become one of the world's most famous advertisements in the *Times* of London in December 1901:

> Men wanted for hazardous journey. Small wages. Bitter cold. Long months of complete darkness. Constant danger. Safe return doubtful. Honour and recognition in case of success.

He reportedly received 5,000 applications for the position. Clearly, men are looking for adventure, significance, and challenge in their lives. But going on adventures means facing dangers. And danger makes us fearful. And being afraid is uncomfortable for most men, and so we shy away from it rather than face down our fear. Weakness keeps us from reaching for greatness.

When I started Better Dads ministry a number of years ago, I made a covenant with God. I told God that this was his ministry and that I would just be available for whatever opportunities he placed in my path. I've since found out that that kind of handshake with God can be a bit unnerving, if not downright dangerous. God has placed numerous opportunities and challenges in my path that I have been obliged to accept. Challenges I would never have chosen to attempt on my own. First of all, he has me speaking in public a large percentage of my time. Public speaking is reportedly the number one fear of most people—even greater than death! If you had known me ten years ago, before I became a Christian, you would never in a million years have pegged me as a public speaker. Then he has put me in opportunities to speak to groups that would not be my first choice: men in prison convicted of assault, murder and rape; women who live alternative lifestyles; adversarial, liberal radio hosts; and other uncomfortable, even semi-dangerous situations. Do I still get apprehensive or even a little afraid when these opportunities arise? Absolutely. Yet, with faith I know that God will protect me, and so I eagerly leap forward (well, maybe cautiously walk forward) despite my trepidations. And God always does perform miracles through (or despite) my weaknesses. It is exhilarating, frightening, and gratifying all at the same time.

But hear me very clearly here—never, *never* have I regretted a moment of the challenges and risks that God placed me in. They give my life meaning and purpose. God wants to use you mightily! But he can't (or more likely won't) until you set aside your weakness and fear of the unknown and allow him the opportunity to use you. Weakness causes us to doubt ourselves (as well as God)—it paralyzes us into inaction. I meet so many men with the potential for greatness within them, and they waste it because they are weak and afraid to take risks. They wallow in their safety and security. Stand up and step out! When God uses you, he gives you a mighty strength that you can feel flow through your soul, energizing your entire being with power and passion.

I implore you, do not be one of those men who at the end of his life has huge regrets and wonders what could have been. Go out and grab life by the *cojones*. Live life with vision and passion—your wife and kids will thank you and you will be blessed mightily.

Self-Indulgence

I was a hard man when I was younger. I was hard on myself and hard on others. I prided myself on never shedding a tear for twenty years of my adult life. But what I discovered was that what I considered "toughness" was really a form of self-indulgence. It allowed me to ignore or discount issues or other people I didn't want to deal with—issues that if I was being honest with myself, I was scared to address. Issues like what I was feeling emotionally, what I needed to change about myself in order to meet my wife's needs, or how I needed to face and heal old wounds that were negatively affecting me even as an adult.

We waste so much energy on self-indulgence, whether through pornography, lust, addictions, or even just video games and movies. Think of what we could accomplish if we put those distractions aside and focused that astounding male energy on constructive pursuits. Heck, thinking about sex alone probably occupies a significant portion of the working areas of most of our brains. If our brains are like computers, then lust is a large application program that hogs the resources of the whole computer, thus slowing down all the other applications and functions.

Another area I notice men indulge themselves is *not accepting responsibility* for their own actions. I once hired a design engineer to develop a new website for our firm. After six months of delays and being ninety days late on the agreed-upon deadline, he still had not produced a finished product. Yet he vehemently protested that it was all somehow my fault. He took no responsibility for his lack of performance. When we act this way (never admitting we are wrong) with our families, it causes irreparable damage to relationships.

Perhaps part of this character flaw in men is due to *false pride*—the pride and competitiveness of always needing to be right and never letting anyone else get the upper hand. But pride (and competitiveness), like many things in life, can be good or bad. Healthy pride helps give us self-esteem; unhealthy pride can cause us to destroy our friends, families, and business relationships.

Another area that many men struggle with is *procrastination*. Men who procrastinate choose the easier path even when they know they should take the road less traveled. They justify it by telling themselves they are just doing what everyone else is doing. The well-traveled path is always easier at the beginning, but you always pay for it down the road. Whenever I put something off that I know I should do, it always comes back to haunt me at some point in the future.

Being self-focused is another indulgence. I know I spend a significant portion of my time and energies trying to satisfy my own needs and wants. Many men I meet struggle with being oblivious to everything around them except what pertains to their own little world. This selfishness pushes us away from manhood. Our innate self-centeredness tells us that I must get *my* needs met before I can meet anyone else's.

Men who allow themselves the luxury of self-indulgence are blindly walking through the jungle of life. They are stepping into quicksand and don't even know it.

A Challenge

Here's what I'd like to challenge you with. Choose one—just one—of the traits mentioned above that you might struggle with. Think about it for several days or weeks and pray that God would give you some insight on how to overcome your inclination toward any of these stumbling blocks of masculinity. Then slowly, one small step at a time, start making changes that force you to face this trait. Keep your steps small. That way if you fall it doesn't hurt as much. But be sure to congratulate yourself and relish your successes when you do something out of your comfort zone.

Before long you will look back and realize you have taken a giant stride forward in your manhood. That is when you will begin walking a little taller and a little stronger. That is when people will start looking to you as a leader and a man.

10

The Godfather

THERE MAY HAVE been no more rugged, masculine man in the Bible than David. One time when he was a teenage shepherd boy, a bear made off with one of his flock. David tracked it down and killed it with just his bare hands to get his sheep back! Another time he did the same with a lion! Think about that, killing bears and lions without a weapon! Being a hunter, I've seen firsthand what each of those animals can do. Given a choice, I don't know if I would be man enough to tackle either of those predators with just my bare hands. Truth be told, I might not be too thrilled about it even with a weapon. Then, as if those accomplishments weren't enough, while still a teenager, he killed a heavily armed nine-foot-tall giant with a bad attitude, using just a sling and a rock, while all the rest of the army of grown men and hardened warriors trembled with fear in a ditch behind him.

He was a great friend. He inspired Jonathan, the son of King Saul, to love him more than a brother. Jonathan looked up to David so much that he willingly gave over his birthright to the throne of the land in order that David could be king. He even risked his life to help save David the many times Jonathan's father tried to kill him.

David was an awesome warrior—his faith in God inspired him to attempt feats that normal men were scared to even think about. He inspired men to follow him unto death. And these weren't just any men—they were the bravest and fiercest warriors in the whole kingdom. David had an inner circle of the mightiest warriors in the kingdom called his "Mighty Men." The leaders of that group were the top three warriors in the entire land. Two of them had each single-handedly killed three hundred men at one time. These men were so inspired by David's leadership that they followed him everywhere, even living in caves when King Saul had a bounty on his head. David inspired such loyalty in his men that three of the Mighty Men snuck into the enemy army's heavily fortified camp just to get him a drink of water when he complained of being thirsty.

David was a real man's man. And yet he was flawed. He made many mistakes. He wasn't necessarily a good husband. He committed adultery and then had the woman's husband killed by sending him into a battle that he could not survive. He wasn't necessarily the best father around. One of his sons tried to overthrow him as king and have him killed. He wasn't the holiest man to walk the face of the earth. He was often scared and frustrated with God. But David had great faith in God and cried out to him in his fear, pain, frustration, anguish, and joy. He also had a repentant heart. God called him a "man after my own heart." David shows us that even if we are imperfect men, reliance on God can make us men who can change history.

Every man has a variety of roles in life to fulfill. The following is a short list of perhaps the most important roles that a man fulfills during his lifetime.

Father

> A man who doesn't spend time with his family can never be a real man.
>
> Don Vito Corleone, *The Godfather*

Short of God's direct intervention, I don't know if a male can achieve all the benefits of full manhood until he becomes a father. I don't mean just fathering a child—any adult male can do that. I mean actually raising one and being responsible for another human being's life. I think it completes a man and matures him in ways that he cannot attain without going through the self-sacrifice that fathering requires. Fathering may be the most significant role a man can perform in his life. But the responsibilities of being a father have evolved over time. For far too long, men were taught that being a father was just putting bread on the table and a roof over their children's heads. But our children also need the emotional, nurturing "father food" that men provide.

My friend Jon tells a compelling story about his father. Jon's father was a typical man of his generation, raised to believe that a father's only role was to provide financially and to protect his family. He did not show much emotion and certainly no affection toward his family, especially his son.

169

His gruff demeanor was a wall he erected to protect himself from the muddy and confusing waters of relationships and their entangled emotions.

While away at college, Jon heard a speaker talk about the need to demonstrate physical affection to those you love regardless of whether they reciprocate or not. Jon vowed the next time he went home he would kiss and hug his father. The first few times he did his father jerked away and was very uncomfortable—he never did seem to warm up to the physical affection his son forced upon him. However, Jon continued to demonstrate his love for his father.

One day Jon's trip home coincided with the visit of one of his father's childhood friends, a man who had raised three sons himself. As his father walked him out to his car to leave, Jon embraced him in a hug and kissed him on the cheek. Jon got into his car and drove back to school. When his father went back into the house, he found his friend crying. Inquiring what was wrong, his friend looked at him and replied, "I would give anything if just one of my sons would hug and kiss me!"

Jon's father reassessed his attitude about the value of his son's demonstration of love. Today Jon's children always go to Grandpa and give him a hug and a kiss. They know that despite his gruff exterior, he is really an old softy.

I think many of us choose not to show our emotions or physical affection because it is safer. Emotions are powerful if not controlled. We are afraid of what will happen if we loosen our grip on these untamable and unpredictable facets of our personalities. Do real men hug and kiss their kids? I believe so.

Perhaps the biggest bane on our culture is the emergence of fatherlessness. The destruction it has done to our children and families is directly responsible for literally every problem we face as a culture. It is especially devastating to males. It is a curse that is passed down from generation to generation, destroying men and women in each successive generation. Even the Son of God needed an earthly father to protect him and provide for him while he was a child.

I speak with men in prison who tell me that, for as far back as many of them can remember, there have never been any men actively present in their family lineage; that there has never been a father in the home for generations. In fact, many men in prison tell me their fathers are also in prison. One man told me he actually met his father for the first time when they brought him to the prison as his cell mate.

Here's what James Lee Burke says about men like these in his novel, *The Tin Roof Blowdown*: "They were raised by their grandmothers and didn't have a clue who their fathers were. They got turned in jail and thought of sexual roles in terms of prey or predator. They lied instinctively, even when there was no reason to. . . . They were inured to insult, indifferent to their own fate, and devoid of guilt or shame. What bothered Clete most about them was his belief that anyone from their background would probably turn out the same."[1]

Millions of men of the past several generations have been and are being raised with the legacy of father abandonment in one form or another. They in turn fulfill their destiny by abandoning their own families, and the cycle continues until an intervention by another male or group of males helps these boys and men break the cycle.

So much of what we are as men is tied up in what we do and what we accomplish. Today, this generally revolves around money. Hence, being a doctor or lawyer has more prestige than being a factory worker or shoe salesman. So, is a man who makes more money or who accomplishes things valued as important by our society more of a man? There are no Super Bowls of fatherhood where the press heaps accolades on the winners, and yet there is no more important job in the universe than that of "dad." It angers me that we're so quick to judge by status and prestige.

I encounter this attitude regularly when I meet new people. When I'm just a "regular old guy," nobody pays special attention to me. Then when they find out I am a published author, their whole demeanor instantly changes. Suddenly, I'm somebody they need to know; I'm important. To me it speaks volumes about their character—if I was not important when I was a "nobody," why am I all of a sudden important because I'm an author? Why am I suddenly more "valuable" than I was when I was *just* a good husband and father?

Many men have been wounded by damaged fathers or by having had no positive male role model to learn under. We stagger and stumble through life, searching for roles and behaviors that fit comfortably enough to survive, all the while yearning for we know not what.

I have spoken with numerous directors of homeless shelters and domestic abuse shelters, and every one of them tells me that, upon reflection, fathers are at the root of all their clients' problems. One woman told me, "I've worked in this industry for thirty-six years. Now that I think about it, every single one of my clients had either no father or an abusive father." Think about that statement the next time you feel unappreciated in your role as a father.

My friend, Marvin Charles, director of D.A.D.S. ministry, once told me, "The AIDS virus does not actually kill anyone.

EFFECTS OF FATHERLESSNESS

- 63% of youth suicides are from fatherless homes.
  Source: U.S. D.H.H.S., Bureau of the Census

- 90% of all homeless and runaway children are from fatherless homes.
  Source: U.S. D.H.H.S., Bureau of the Census

- 85% of all children that exhibit behavioral disorders come from fatherless homes.
  Source: Centers for Disease Control

- 80% of rapists motivated with displaced anger come from fatherless homes.
  Source: Criminal Justice & Behavior, Vol. 14, 403–26, 1978

- 71% of all high school dropouts come from fatherless homes.
  Source: National Principals Association Report
  on the State of High Schools

- 75% of all adolescent patients in chemical abuse centers come from fatherless homes.
  Source: Rainbows For All God's Children

- 70% of juveniles in state-operated institutions come from fatherless homes.
  Source: U.S. Dept. of Justice, Special Report, September 1988

These statistics translate to mean that children from a fatherless home are:

- 5 times more likely to commit suicide
- 32 times more likely to run away
- 20 times more likely to have behavioral disorders
- 14 times more likely to commit rape
- 9 times more likely to drop out of high school
- 10 times more likely to abuse chemical substances
- 9 times more likely to end up in a state-operated institution
- 20 times more likely to end up in prison[2]

The virus just lowers your bodily defenses so that other infections can invade the body, which is what actually causes death. Fatherlessness is like AIDS. Fatherlessness does not actually kill the family; it just lowers the defenses so other issues can infect it, eventually destroying it."

We all yearn for the respect and approval of our fathers. We all crave the love and understanding of a father or father figure. Many men have told me that the most important aspect in their journey from boyhood to manhood was when they finally felt they had earned the respect of their fathers. But children also need love and forgiveness modeled from their fathers—the same love and forgiveness that our heavenly Father gives to each of us.

Ernest Hemingway, in his short story "The Capital of the World," tells of a father and his teenage son who lived in Spain. Their relationship became strained and his son ran away from home. The father began a long journey in search of the lost and rebellious son, finally putting an ad in the Madrid newspaper as a last resort. His son's name was Paco, a very common name in Spain. The ad simply read: "Dear Paco, meet me in front of the Hotel Montana tomorrow at noon. All is forgiven, Papa."

As Hemingway writes, the next day at noon in front of the hotel there were eight hundred sons named Paco who were all seeking the forgiveness of a loving father.[3]

Provider

> Becoming Father the Nurturer rather than just Father the Provider enables a man to fully feel and express his humanity and his masculinity. Fathering is the most masculine thing a man can do.
>
> Frank Pittman, *Man Enough*

Providing for our children is one of the earliest and most basic roles that men have fulfilled. For most of human history, it was the man's role to hunt and provide sustenance for his family. After hunter/gatherers phased out, men farmed; and after the industrial revolution, they went to work in factories, but always under the umbrella of providing. This role is ingrained in us as men to the point that if we do not provide, it often affects us in profound ways. But sometimes providing consists of more than just working longer or harder.

I owned a relatively successful business for the sixteen years before going into full-time ministry. A year and a half into the ministry, finances became a challenge—a real challenge! It meant having to step out in faith for God's daily provision, which was definitely a growth experience for me and my wife. It nearly stretched me beyond what I was capable of enduring. To support ourselves until revenue began coming in, we spent all of our savings, investments, and retirement accounts—a lifetime of work invested in a dream that was my vision. This was probably not as difficult for me as it was for my wife. As a man, it probably would not have been as hard on me to lose our home and live in a shack in pursuit of my dreams, but my wife had raised a family in the security of our home. During this time of walking by faith, she had to rely on my vision alone, while I was convinced beyond a shadow of a doubt that God was calling me to this ministry and that he would provide. I remember my teenage daughter being very concerned when I closed my business and went into full-time ministry. She asked, "Daddy, how are we going to make it? What will we do for money?"

I said, "Well, honey, I believe that God will provide for us."

To which she somewhat desperately responded, "But what if he doesn't?"

I told her, "I guess we'll worry about that when the time comes."

After a year and a half, that time had come. We literally were down to nothing. No money; nothing to fall back on.

I felt like I was not fulfilling my role as a man to provide for my family. Even though God was meeting our needs on a day-to-day basis, it was very stressful and, if I'm truthful, a little humiliating.

One day the thought popped into my head, "You know . . . you have a big life insurance policy. But you are not currently making much money. The truth is, you are worth more dead than alive."

The more I thought about that, the more it started to ring true. It seemed to become an obsessive thought over the next several weeks. Perhaps I *was* worth more dead than alive.

One day after a strenuous "discussion" over finances with Suzanne, we went for a walk together. I finally bolstered my courage and shared with her the thoughts I had been having about being worth more dead than alive.

Suzanne stopped dead in her tracks and started crying. She then shared with me that she had been consumed with the thought, "I am not making Rick happy. Hence, I was a bad wife and my family would be better off if I were dead."

We both instantly realized where these thoughts were coming from. They were being whispered in our ear by the evil one. He was attacking us in the area where we were being most effective for God—in our family. He was trying to take us out of the "game." And he nearly succeeded.

My obsession with "providing" for my family in the way *I* thought I should be instead of relying on God was very nearly my undoing. While it is a man's responsibility to financially provide for his wife and any children he brings into this world (even if he never gets to see them), God very often has plans that are so much bigger than anything we might be able to see.

I recognize now that the struggles we went through, while perhaps not a test, were designed to grow our faithfulness and to teach us lessons we needed to learn in order to succeed with the ministry. Today, we are reaping the benefits of God's blessings for that faithfulness and perseverance. Perhaps the best lessons in this trial were that my wife's faith in me and my vision was proven, and my faith in God was rewarded for my daughter to see firsthand.

Protector

> When men are not men, a civilization falls.
>
> Stu Weber, *Four Pillars of a Man's Heart*

Many a time I've prowled around the house in the middle of the night, checking on the sleeping children, making sure the doors and windows were locked, and staring off into the darkness wondering how best to keep my family safe and secure—all the while thinking about how to juggle the bills to ensure that everything was paid even when the funds weren't there. Thinking about my children's health and my wife's happiness.

One of a man's most basic roles in life is to protect his family. It wasn't too long ago that a father was required to face danger from marauding bandits, wild animals, or warring tribes in order to physically protect his family. Sometimes protection is easy to identify, other times less so. If someone physically threatens his wife or children, most men will (or should) come at them like an enraged lion. Certainly, if someone said something rude or offensive to or about his wife, or threatened to harm his child, most men would take immediate action. That's clearly an overt threat to his wife and children.

But what about a threat that is less obvious? What about allowing into your home a saturation of music and videos, movies and television shows that clearly mean harm to the psychological, spiritual, and emotion well-being of your child? Do we just turn away because it's too big of a battle to fight? Think for a moment about older times, perhaps back in the pioneer days. If a man or group of men came into town and started using inappropriate, offensive, sexually graphic language and violent behavior in front of women and children, would the men of the town just stand by and do nothing? No, they would have run the offenders out of town on a rail. What is different today? An entertainment industry corrupts the innocence and moral value system of our children in order to make money, and we allow it. Oftentimes we don't make the effort to fight it because it is uncomfortable or requires too much time and energy.

While my daughter Kelsey was dating in high school, I made it a practice to meet with her suitors individually for lunch. This allowed me to check them out and to have the "talk" with them. This tended to eliminate many young men who would not be desirable for her to date (in my humble opinion). There are too many other unprotected young women out there for them to prey upon. My reputation soon preceded me. One young man who had a longtime crush on her finally asked her to dinner. She replied, "You mean, like a date?"

After a brief pause, he responded, "No, I don't think I'm quite ready yet to have lunch with your dad."

Kelsey is nineteen years old now and living in her own apartment. She was home visiting the other day and was telling me about all the young men who are enamored with her and want to date her. I somewhat jokingly suggested she have the young men call me to schedule a lunch. But after thinking about it a moment I told her, "Kelsey, you are nineteen years old now, an adult living on your own. I guess I don't need to interview your dates any longer."

She thought about it for a minute and said, "That's okay—you can still do it!" I thought to myself as I mentally pumped my fist in the air, *Yes! She understands!* My heart swelled to realize that I had gotten it right. She realized the value of having a father who loved her and was willing to protect her. I can only imagine the feelings of safety and security that produces in a young woman.

When I tell the men I speak to in prison that research indicates 60 to 80 percent of children with an incarcerated parent will themselves wind up in the criminal justice system, they are stunned.[4] It is as if no one ever explained to them the model they set for their children is followed so closely. They never recognized the influence they have in the lives of their children. No one ever told them that they can protect their children from many of life's failures merely by the model they provide and the example they show.

A man also has a duty to protect others, especially those who cannot protect themselves. While I think most of us instinctively know that, what does it look like in real life?

On sunny days (which are only about three months out of the year here in the beautiful Pacific Northwest) I like to either walk or ride my bike during lunch hours. I travel along a former railroad line that has been converted and paved into a pedestrian walking/biking trail called the Springwater Trail. The Springwater Trail is a twenty-six-mile trail that skirts the perimeter of the east side of Portland from the small hamlet of Corbett to the east banks of the Willamette River in downtown Portland. Much of the trail in my area is somewhat rural in location with trees, bushes, wildlife, and blackberries lining both sides of the trail. Many people use the trail, but transients have been known to camp in the woods, and I've seen some pretty disreputable-looking characters gathered in such spots. It doesn't seem like a very safe environment for women or children, but you'd be surprised at how many of each I see roaming around alone even at dawn or dusk. This may seem a little corny, but whenever I am on the trail, I always consider anyone on the trail (especially women or children) as being under my protection. Sort of like a lawman in the Old West. For as far as I can see, while I'm on the trail, whoever is there is under my protection.

My wife and I were in Alaska on a speaking tour several years ago. After speaking to a group of women at a local church one evening, I was struck with the urgent need to wait until everyone was gone before leaving. Everyone had left the building except two women who were cleaning up. Even though I was exhausted and suffering from a terrible head cold, I made the driver of our car wait in the parking lot until they were done before leaving. Shortly before the ladies left, a nasty-looking car slowly idled into the lot and waited several minutes facing the door as if to see who was in the building. I could not see who was in the car, but after they noticed us waiting, they slowly pulled away and left the premises. Perhaps it was nothing, but I shudder to think of how I would have felt had I selfishly left and something terrible happened to those two wonderful ladies.

Husband

You know, the finest line a man will walk is between success
at work and success at home. I have a motto: Like your work,
love your wife.

Del Griffith, *Planes, Trains, and Automobiles*

I wish I could say that after twenty-seven years of marriage
I have all the answers to creating and maintaining a healthy,
happy marriage. But that would be a lie. Sometimes I think
I'm a pretty good husband; other times I know I fall miserably
short of adequate. I still spend more time thinking about my
own needs and desires than I do my wife's. I still hurt her
feelings on a semi-regular basis with my insensitivity. And
I still don't know and understand her nearly as well as she
does me. Even after all this time, women are still a bit of an
enigma to me.

It strikes me that perhaps of all the roles I undertake in life,
I am most inadequate in this one—or at least I feel that way.
This role may well be the most difficult one I attempt, even
more difficult than being a father. I admit that, like all men,
I don't always treat my wife as well as she deserves. Frankly
sometimes I'm just too selfish and prideful to bend my will
in order to meet her needs. But she needs my understanding
and consideration in our everyday relationship.

Your wife is created to desperately need and desire a close
relationship with you. But the daily distractions that we focus
on as men often pull us away from giving her the nonsexual
intimacy she needs. She needs to feel honored and loved by
us, just as much or more than we need to feel admired and
respected by her. She needs to be frequently reassured of our
love for her. That concept has always been a little difficult

for me to understand, but I know it to be true nonetheless. Women seem to value words more than men do. And so, even though I might feel like my actions are expressing my love for her, she still needs to hear that I love and cherish her through my words—frequently. Again, as men we have been equipped to powerfully give honor to those under our care and guidance. Our wives should be the first person we make sure is continually blessed by this influence we have been given.

Remember too that love is a decision, not a feeling. Love is an action, not an emotion. So if you do the actions and behaviors that exhibit love for your wife, your feelings will naturally follow. I can't tell you how many times I've been unhappy with my wife, but once I started treating her with honor, my feelings changed to ones of love almost instantly.

I've noticed that my wife tends to fret or worry about things over which she has no control or responsibility. She even feels guilty about those areas in which she has no control. She will do things for everyone else, sometimes to the detriment of her health and stamina. I don't know if these traits are true with all wives, but I suspect that every woman needs our masculine support to some degree in order to "let go" of these areas.

Here's another thing you need to know: seeking counseling is not unmanly. If you are struggling with issues either personally or in your marriage, it is your responsibility to find counseling, not to wait for your wife to insist upon it. Part of being a leader is keeping ourselves healthy and making decisions based on what's best for our families. If you are hurting, angry, frustrated, or anxious, go see a counselor—it's okay.

So I guess the best advice I can give for this role of a man's life is to be understanding of your wife's needs and then diligent in recognizing that they need to be met on an ongoing, consistent basis. If you do that, it will make all the other roles you need to fulfill in life a whole lot easier.

Champion

> Defend the poor and the fatherless;
> Do justice to the afflicted and needy.
> Deliver the poor and needy;
> Free them from the hand of the wicked.
>
> Psalm 82:3–4 NKJV

The movie *Antwone Fisher* is about an angry young man about to be forcibly discharged from the Navy. Born in a women's prison, Antwone is angry because he never met his father and had been abandoned by his mother as a baby into a foster care system of sexual abuse and pain. He finds an unlikely advocate in the form of a Navy psychiatrist, Jerome Davenport, with a sympathetic heart who not only counsels Antwone but also mentors him and provides the father figure he never had—an older man who loves and cares for him. Antwone wrote and gave Davenport a poem in gratitude for his help. It sums up his feelings, and those of many fatherless young men, of pain, fear, frustration, and anxiety. He wrote it through the lens of a little boy who is abandoned, lost, and hurt, a boy who tried so hard to be good. It repeatedly asks the fundamental question, "Who will cry for the little boy?"

Davenport starts to read it and Fisher quietly recites the rest of the poem from memory. As he finishes the poem, the scene concludes like this:

Antwone Fisher: ". . . Who will cry for the little boy, who cries inside of me."

Jerome Davenport: Who will cry for the little boy, Antwone?

Antwone Fisher: I will. I always do.[5]

In this movie, Denzel Washington (who played Jerome Davenport) was a champion for Antwone Fisher. He took the time and effort to lift him up, to help teach him what he needed to know in order to succeed in life instead of self-destructing as he was programmed to do. He lifted him up and then pushed him forward into the next stage of his life. He was his champion. A man who used his God-given power and influence to rescue a young man who otherwise would have ended up dead or in prison. It's what men are supposed to do.

One of my most favorite events that our ministry puts on each year is the Single Moms Family Camp. Every summer we go to a beautiful ranch out in the middle of nowhere, and put on a free camp just for single moms and their kids. During this three-day event, the moms participate in a number of life-changing classes, but mostly they are pampered and served. During the day their kids spend time with a group of men who do things with them like horseback riding, carpentry, playing in the creek, and chopping wood—ranch kind of stuff. Things that kids from the city with single moms seldom get to do. We all come together for meals and in the evening for special events. We have time to reflect on the day's events around a campfire. We then have Cowboy Church on Sunday morning.

A number of mature Christian women also volunteer to be mentors and to pray with the moms when things we study hit too close to home (things like the role their fathers played in the choices they make today; why they choose the types of men they are attracted to; and the fact that God loves them regardless of what they look like, how much they weigh, and what kind of mistakes they've made). These women also serve the moms. Last year they washed their feet and gave them pedicures. Many of the moms were embarrassed because they were not used to being honored this way. During exit interviews with the moms after the camp, they made tearful comments such as, "I have never felt actually 'seen' before," "This is the first time my kids have ever witnessed me being valued as a person," and "This experience has changed my life and the life of my children."

One of the biggest benefits the moms reported for them and their children was merely seeing a healthy relationship modeled between the husbands and wives who volunteer to serve at the camp. They say that they or their children are rarely exposed to something like this.

The men and women who volunteer to help put this camp on are champions to these widows and orphans of our culture. They are making a huge difference in the lives of these families, possibly helping to break generational cycles of abuse, abandonment, and even addictions.

Everyone deserves a champion in their lives, someone who will give them a hand up when they are down, someone who believes in them even when everyone else ignores them, someone who will teach them what they don't know in order to help them change their lives. I think God chose men to be champions in people's lives.

Men can be champions to other men. A while back, my publisher asked me to write a book for women, which ended up being *The Man Whisperer*. I was really struggling with the content and format of the book. As I was discussing it with my agent, Greg Johnson (no relation), he told me something that made a difference in my life: "Just start writing, Rick. You are a very good writer. Your best book is still in you."

His words instantly inspired me. He could have chosen to say basically the same thing, only in a non-uplifting way. He could have said, "Well, do the best you can. You're still learning as a writer." But that would have focused on the negative instead of the positive. It would have deflated me instead of inspiring me. Greg has a lot of experience in publishing, and having him tell me I was a very good writer was a big boost to my self-confidence. Greg used his power and influence to lift me up instead of tearing me down. On that day, he was my champion when I really needed one.

Conclusion

God created us to make the lives of others better and more abundant. To do that, we have to be healthy, authentic, and confident in our role as men. Thus we have an obligation to ourselves and to those who depend upon us to recognize our wounds and shortcomings. We can then begin to heal from them. Each of us does the things we do for a reason—we never just do something or make a decision without a reason. It may be an illogical or unhealthy reason, but it's a reason nonetheless. We must find out what prompts us to act the way we do so that we can change destructive habits and focus on healthy behaviors to model for our children and others who are influenced by us. In order to fulfill the roles in life that matter to so many people, we must understand our influence and power and then fulfill those roles to the best of our ability.

Why? Because without us, people will die or live lives of poverty and despair.

11

The Adventures of Indiana Jones

ADVENTURE

Life is hard; it's harder if you're stupid.

John Wayne

IN THE MOVIE *Tears of the Sun*, as civil war rages in the African country of Nigeria, US citizens are stuck in the war-torn country. Muslim rebels have just assassinated the presidential family and are on a rampage throughout the country performing an "ethnic cleansing" by killing the other tribes. Bruce Willis is in command of a team of Special-Ops soldiers sent in to retrieve an American doctor (who just coincidently happens to be a beautiful woman). After arriving at her clinic, she refuses to leave unless seventy refugees are taken to safe haven with them. The priest and the nuns want to stay, and the doctor will come only if the Nigerian refugees can come too. Willis initially agrees, only to leave the refugees behind at the drop zone as soon as the doctor is on the helicopter. Then, from the helicopter, he witnesses the results of the rebels' destruction of the surrounding countryside and its people, and in an instant he disobeys his orders and turns the helicopter around.

Willis's character, a fiercely loyal man, decides that the only way to complete the mission is to save them too. They begin a foot race across the Nigerian jungle with ruthless rebels chasing them, in an attempt to lead the refugees to the border of Cameroon. His group must trek the jungles with no assistance and three hundred Nigerian rebels hot on their trail. Along the way, they encounter a village under siege by a group of the rebels. The men of the village have been brutally murdered and the women raped. The rebels engage in crimes against humanity, acts of mutilation and torture.

Most of the soldiers sacrifice their lives through heroic effort to get the group of refugees to safety. One of the refugees is the former king's son, the heir to the throne. His rescue brings hope to the thousands of refugees at the border camp. Willis's character develops through the duration of the movie from a hardened soldier to a complex, caring character focused on saving the refugees. He and his soldiers are men to be admired.

All good "guy" movies have several things in common: sexy women, lots of adventure and action, and good eventually triumphing over evil after a mighty battle. Let's look at the role each of these factors plays in authentic masculinity.

The Influence of Women on Masculinity

The movies generally portray a "real" man as having sex with a variety of attractive women. But in reality, a guy could have sex with a lot of women and still not be authentically masculine. It's been my experience that women don't often understand authentic masculinity very well. So if you judge yourself by what women think (and your success with them sexually), instead of what other men think—especially authentically masculine men—you're deluding yourself. Males need the affirmation and validation of an older male (not a female) whom they look up to in order to finally grow and mature into authentic masculinity.

At some point, boys must break away from the tightly wrapped arms of motherhood in order to achieve true masculinity. They must make a break from the world of women. And men must recognize that they cannot rely on women to hand them the crown of masculinity.

I have a friend, an ex-NBA player, who grew up in the projects of an urban city. He was raised by women—a mother and three sisters. He shared with me that one of the biggest problems he faced as he became a man was that he was never taught healthy coping skills by a man. He had only female influences early in life, and so he found himself frustrated and angry in stressful situations. He had learned to make decisions based on his feelings. Because he couldn't channel his emotions properly, he made irrational choices that led to consequences like being kicked off his high school basketball team despite being an All-American and then losing a full-ride college scholarship by fighting with his coach. The problem followed him into the NBA because the players are generally surrounded only by yes-men—no one ever tells them when they are wrong. It was only by finding some strong male mentors and role models to help guide him that he was able to turn his life around. Today he devotes his life to helping young men understand what it takes to be successful by giving them hope and knowledge.

The more a man allows a woman (mother, wife, girlfriend) to define his masculinity, the less of a man he will be. Why? Because a woman is not a man—she cannot empower masculinity. A man has to follow his male instincts instead of following a female's direction of what a man is and what his role should entail.

Women do play a role in developing masculinity in our culture, though. Women in a society influence the *type* of men a culture creates merely by those men they choose to have sex with. Men conform to the requirements and rules to which they are held accountable. This applies to relationships just as much as the business or sports world. Bottom line, the character of the men a woman sleeps with encourages that character in all men. If enough women have sex with men of low character, that is what all men will aspire to be like. If they sleep only with men of noble character, then that is the standard all men will strive to live up to. Either way, their offspring (male and female) will tend to follow in those footsteps modeled for them.[1]

Unfortunately, many women are notoriously poor judges of what constitutes authentic masculinity. All you have to do is look around at all the women who have chosen men who abandoned or abused them or used them purely for their own self-gratification.

In the movie *Casablanca*, Victor (played by Paul Heinrich) is a heroic and virtuous leader of men. Even though married to this noble man, his wife Ilsa, played by Ingrid Bergman, ends up choosing Rick (Humphrey Bogart), a man who readily admits that he lives life only for himself.

So how does this all work and why are we driven to compete for the attention of women as a badge of our masculinity? Most men are performance-based creatures. We are trained to be that way. Because we are programmed (hard-wired) to reproduce with as many of the most beautiful women as possible, and because women are wired to strive for security by mating with the best provider (survival of a species compels the most powerful males to mate with the most beautiful females), we tend to base the "success" of our masculinity on how well we perform materially. The better we perform, the more women are interested in us. It's why even older men can act like fools over a young, pretty girl. Men compete for the most beautiful women by "performing" against each other. The more beautiful a woman a man can "have" (marry or have sex with), the more status he has within the male community. There are exceptions to this rule of using beautiful women as an elevation of our status, of course. Men will happily "settle" for other attributes if they feel they cannot compete for beautiful women. Today, this performance standard tends to be based on how much money we earn and how many material goods we can accumulate. That generally determines how many women we can "earn," thus determining our success as men. It is a vicious circle which we cannot escape.

I know some people will take umbrage over this generalization of men (and women), but even if he's fat, rude, and ignorant, you seldom see a rich man with an ugly woman.

Authentic masculinity, though, recognizes the folly of this cycle and judges itself on other factors than just what our culture dictates. It recognizes that women are not just objects to be judged solely on their physical appearance. It allows a man to judge himself and his masculinity by a higher standard of performance than making money in order to bed women. That performance standard is one that uses its power and influence to make the lives of those around him better and more enriched. His goal then is to use his masculine performance to "earn" respect and admiration from his wife so that he is more capable of honoring and cherishing her.

Men of Action and Adventure

> Most men lead lives of quiet desperation and go to the grave with the song still in them.
>
> Henry David Thoreau

If there is one verse ever written specifically for men in the Bible it may be 1 Corinthians 16:13, which says, "Be on guard; stand firm in the faith; be men of courage; be strong." Those words are a powerful calling to a man's heart.

To be on guard is to be aware of what is going on around us—to understand the deeper implications of what is happening. This requires vigilance and a certain amount of wisdom. We need to guard our hearts and be aware of potential dangers for those under our protection. Being on guard calls to a man's heart as a protector.

Standing firm in your faith requires having values and convictions you believe in, and then standing behind those convictions even in the face of adversity. It requires you to have resolve and faith. It requires what the old-timers used to refer to as "having sand." It means standing by your convictions despite your surroundings and circumstances.

Be a man. Act like a man. Stop acting like a woman. That really says it all. Sometimes I get to feeling sorry for myself or get tired and start whining about stuff. When that happens, I always watch an inspirational guy movie to snap me back into my role and duty as a man. Or if none are available, I just forcefully tell myself, *Stop it! Act like a man—be a man!* It tends to put things back into perspective for me. Most men struggle to find that fine line between being able to "suck it up" and being whiny. Too far in one direction and you end up an emotionally frozen robot; too far the other way and you end up being a wuss. Cultivate masculine traits such as courage, honor, integrity, and loyalty. It takes courage to be a man today. Acting like a man makes you think and feel like a man.

Be strong! What a simple yet empowering statement. I would propose that men are at their strongest when they are helping others—lifting them up to be more than they could possibly be without them in their lives. But several issues detract from a man's ability to do this.

For one thing, Christian culture especially tends to be appearance driven. Hence, if you look good and act good (at least in public), then you are somehow more holy and a better Christian—you are more accepted anyway. That encourages many men to strive for a kind of behavioral perfection. But behavioral perfection is a dangerous game for men. We all make mistakes (some of us guys make a lot of them). It is impossible to achieve perfection in our behaviors. So pretty soon, because we cannot measure up, we get discouraged and end up quitting the game.

While our behaviors are important and do count, true holiness comes from a *desire* to be Christlike. Look, we all make mistakes. And men do and think stupid things all the time. What's more important than looking good on the outside is a man trying his best, admitting his mistakes when he makes them, and then repenting and taking responsibility for them. That way when we fail (and it is inevitable that we will), we can still receive God's blessings. One of the reasons for the church's failure to connect with men is expecting them to be perfect. This behavioral perfection often translates into eliminating some of the character traits that are most dear to a man's heart, such as boisterousness, competitiveness, healthy aggressiveness, and assertiveness.

When we make mistakes, it is important that we recognize them as such, admit that we made a mistake, learn from it, and then forget about it. If we can do that, then our mistakes will not hold us back from moving forward to help others. We all make mistakes, but that's all they are—they are not the end of our lives nor do they define our lives.

I have a friend who stumbled badly and had an affair that led to a divorce from his wife. One of the hardest things he had to do was tell his teenage son about the entire situation and how badly he had messed up. But once he did that and admitted responsibility, God did an amazing thing. Because he had admitted to his son that he was not perfect, his son suddenly realized he could talk to his dad! He understood that his dad was human and made mistakes. He realized he could come to his dad with his troubles and would not be judged harshly. Today my friend and his son have a wonderful, open relationship that is deeper than it ever would have been had he not admitted his failures to his son. God used his "realness" to bless him and other people.

People connect and relate to people who are just like they are—flawed. Sometimes men are appearance driven and try to look perfect to the outside world. But that façade does not draw people to you—nobody likes or relates to someone who is perfect. But men who have "stature," who carry themselves in a real, authentic way, are very attractive to people. They are open and authentic about their faults. These men are approachable and have the ability to deal with their failures in a healthy way—by not hiding them. And so people are drawn to a man like that, which then allows him to use what he has learned from his experiences to benefit others.

The Battle of Good versus Evil

I'm not sure when I first became comfortable with myself as a man. I think it probably occurred when I healed enough to be able to look at myself in the mirror and like what I saw. I was then able to start helping other people, which in turn tempered, strengthened, and polished my masculinity.

The truth is I think most of us men know deep down what a man is without being told. But the negative forces in our culture and within the spiritual realm that want to destroy masculinity do a good job of either distracting us from our mission or else brainwashing us into believing lies. But when a man sees the character of a "real" man, he recognizes it for what it is and is inspired to follow.

One challenge I was faced with, and I think most men suffer from, is having an "imposter complex." Early on I wasn't confident as a man. I didn't know if I measured up as a husband, a father, and a man. Consequently I was easily intimidated by life. One reason was because at that time I did not have the forgiveness and healing of a loving God. I didn't understand the power that comes with the indwelling of the Holy

Spirit, and that we can "do all things through Christ" (Phil. 4:13 NKJV). I didn't know anything about the power of God's Word to be with us even in our failures.

But after receiving my heavenly Father's blessing of forgiveness, I began to heal from my internal wounds. While my wife seldom criticizes me, if she does, it can feel like a stab in the heart with a dagger—especially if I am feeling insecure already about whatever she mentions. But as I began to think of myself as a good man and good husband, I wasn't intimidated by life or by things that used to devastate me—like criticism from my wife. I was then able to face the world confidently. I knew who I was and what God made me to be. This led to successes. Success is very important to a man. To feel adequate and capable in all he does, to be respected by his wife and have self-respect—these are the things that inspire men to be what God intended.

Success in life is doing all the little things well. Almost everyone does the big things that you need to do to succeed, but hardly anyone pays attention to the small, unpleasant, or inconsequential details. If you want to be successful, work hard and do *everything* to the best of your ability. Do your best in all areas—do the ordinary things better than everyone else. So many people are their own worst enemies. Either because they have a fear of success or because they've been programmed to fail, they seem to sabotage themselves. But champions do not beat themselves. They take pride in all they do and always look for ways to improve. Mostly, though, people who succeed submit themselves to God's authority and leadership. By this I mean they pray about decisions before they make them, they understand God's Word, and they recognize God's role for them in life.

Believe me, all those things are easier to talk about, though, than to actually implement in your life.

What Men Admire in Other Men

Men admire certain traits in other men. They admire confidence, leadership, patriarchal bearing, vision for generations, and initiative. Men admire other men who are dependable, honorable, and considerate, and who fight for what's right. They admire men who are good family men, responsible, and caring. And they admire men who attempt and strive for greatness. I've noticed that even men without those characteristics secretly look up to men who have them.

So how come some men attain greatness while thousands of their peers wallow in mediocrity? Is it fate, karma, luck, or even destiny? I don't think so—all men come with the same basic equipment. Every man who's ever become president of the United States, or cured a disease, or benefited the lives of thousands of his fellow human beings puts his pants on one leg at a time just like you and me. We are all just men. Flawed but created in the image of God.

God planted the seeds of greatness in all of us. It's our job to nurture those seeds, to find the path God has in store for us, to have the courage to step out in faith, and the perseverance to struggle through the difficult times placed in our path. Greatness doesn't necessarily mean being famous. Most great men are mired in obscurity.

My friend Jon is a great man. Everything he does in life, whether at work, at home, at church, anywhere, he does with intentionality to make a difference in someone's life. He quietly goes about his business being a positive influence in every opportunity that presents itself. He helps mentor fatherless boys, he teaches Sunday school, he helps people when they move, he goes on mission trips, he often volunteers his time to help others. Jon uses his masculine power to empower the lives of others. Jon is living a life of greatness. Is Jon famous? No, only to those he helps and to God in heaven.

A Stand-Up Guy Redux

I was having lunch with my friend Dennis the other day. Dennis is a highly decorated Vietnam veteran. I asked him about his experiences in the war. He told me that while he had some horrific moments, he has *chosen* to take the positive lessons from that experience—like leadership, self-sufficiency, perseverance, internal toughness, and fortitude—and use them as a foundation to move forward in life. I admire that quality in Dennis.

Perhaps that best describes what a stand-up guy is really all about. Taking bad circumstances and turning them into positive situations is what a man does. Many people come from bad circumstances—either a bad home life or other conditions beyond their control. It's how we respond to these circumstances that determines our character. When we can take the positives from a situation and move forward instead of allowing the past to hold us back or suck us down, that's when we are able to make a difference in the world.

A man's role is to do what he is supposed to do, not just what he wants to do. When we allow ourselves to follow our compulsions (like drinking beer and chasing twenty-year-old cheerleaders), it leads to destruction. Many men are divorced and have destroyed their families by following their compulsions. Our culture encourages us to satisfy our urges—to fulfill our own needs.

A stand-up guy strives for more than that. He is a man who understands his role in life. He recognizes his God-given authority and power to bless others and uses it for good. He makes a difference in his home, in his community, and maybe even in the world. His masculine "essence" improves and seeps down through the generations like butter on a stack of hotcakes. His having been here made a difference in the world and will make a difference in the lives of people for generations to come. You and I, we're just average guys. But God gave us the ability to influence and change the world. We just have to step up and be stand-up guys.

God bless you on your journey! You and I can make a difference in this world, but we have to stand up and be counted—together, arm in arm, shoulder to shoulder. Never forget, you are a man—you matter!

CONTRACT FOR MEN

    I believe that men were created to live lives of significance. I believe men are born with the magnificent ability to lift up the lives of those around them. I believe authentic masculinity can make a difference in the world. Because I believe that, I agree to abide by and live my life by the following code and to inspire those who follow in my footsteps to join me:

A man is not passive—he takes initiative.

A man uses his God-given influence to serve others.

A man defends those who are weaker than he—he stands for what is right.

A man protects and provides for his family.

A man bases his decisions on principles, not emotions.

A man is a spiritual leader of his family.

A man protects all women and children.

A man teaches those under his influence what he has learned.

A man does not quit—no matter how tough things get.

A man is patient, affirming, kind, and loving to his family.

A man is accountable to God and other men.

Signed_____

Date_____

Notes

Chapter 1 Raging Bull

1. Kent Nerburn, *Letters to My Son: A Father's Wisdom on Manhood, Women, Life and Love* (San Rafael, CA: New World Library, 1994), xvii.

Chapter 2 The Good, the Bad, and the Ugly

1. Gary Smalley and John Trent, PhD, *The Hidden Value of a Man* (Colorado Springs, Focus on the Family Publishing, 1992), 10.

2. Stanford Prison Experiment, http://en.wikipedia.org/wiki/Stanford_prison _experiment.

3. Information on Westley Allan Dodd gleaned from: Crime Library, "Prowling at the the Movies," by Shirley Lynn Scott, http://www.crimelibrary.com/serial_ killers/predators/dodd/movies_1.html; http://www.francesfarmersrevenge.com/ stuff/serialkillers/dodd.htm; and Westley Allan Dodd, "The Vancouver Child-Killer," summarized by Aleisha Branch, Holly Bryan, Maria Giovenco, Nicole Nichols, Elzabeth Yeatts, Department of Psychology, Radford University, http://maamodt .asp.radford.edu/Psyc%20405/serial%20killers/Dodd,%20Westley%20Allan.pdf.

Chapter 3 Gladiator

1. "Masculinity," Wikipedia, http://en.wikipedia.org/wiki/Masculinity.

2. Nathan Scott Jr., "Ernest Hemingway, A Critical Essay," in Linda Wagner, *Ernest Hemingway: Five Decades of Criticism* (Lansing, MI: Michigan State University Press, 1974), 217. Cited in Jim Shoe, "Masculinity in Hemingway," November 25, 2002, http://www.essaydepot.com/essayme/1876/index.php.

3. Robert Penn Warren, "Ernest Hemingway," in Wagner, *Ernest Hemingway*, 79. Cited in Shoe, "Masculinity."

4. Jeffrey Marx, *Season of Life* (New York: Simon & Schuster, 2003), 63–64.

5. *Kingdom of Heaven*, directed by Ridley Scott (Twentieth Century Fox Film Corp., 2005).

6. Rick Johnson, *The Man Whisperer* (Grand Rapids: Revell, 2008).

Chaper 4 Braveheart

1. Section gleaned from "Honor Codes," "Principles," "Ideals," "Honor," Wikipedia, http://en.wikipedia.org/wiki/Honor_code.

2. Old West Legends—The Code of the West, http://www.legendsofamerica .com/WE-CodeOfTheWest.html.

3. Cited in Joe Wheeler, "Why You Should Read Zane Grey," *Points West Chronicle*, Spring–Summer 1996, http://www.zgws.org/zgwsread.html.

4. David Roberts, "The Cowboy's Indians, Waldo Wilcox: Range Creek's Fremont Artifact," *National Geographic*, http://www.nationalgeographic.com/adventure/ photography/united-states/southwest/utah-range-creek/waldo-wilcox.html.

5. Ibid.

Chapter 5 Secondhand Lions

1. Nelson Algren, *A Walk on the Wild Side* (New York: Farrar, Straus & Giroux, 2001), back cover.

2. Donald Miller and John MacMurray, *To Own a Dragon* (Colorado Springs: NavPress, 2006), 34, 49.

3. Rogers Wright and Nicholas Cummings, eds., *Destructive Trends in Mental Health: The Well-Intentioned Path to Harm* (New York: Routledge, 2005).

4. Steve Farrar, *King Me: What Every Son Wants and Needs from His Father* (Chicago: Moody, 2005). This theme runs throughout the book.

Chapter 6 Kelly's Heroes

1. Becky Bohrer, "Katrina Families Settle in Canadaville," *Boston Globe*, Boston. com, June 29, 2007, http://www.boston.com/news/nation/articles/2007/06/29/ katrina_families_settle_in_canadaville/.

2. Victor Frankl, *Man's Search for Meaning* (Boston: Beacon Press, 1959). First published in Germany under the title *Ein Psycholog erlebt das Konzentrationslager*.

Chapter 7 The Magnificent Seven (Plus One)

1. Generally attributed to Frank Outlaw, but there is some debate that Ralph Waldo Emerson is the author.

Chapter 8 The Lord of the Rings

1. Sam Keen, *Fire in the Belly* (New York: Bantam Books, 1991), 46.

Chapter 9 The Dirty (Half) Dozen

1. Paul Coughlin, *No More Christian Nice Guy* (Bloomington, MN: Bethany, 2005). Entire section inspired by information gleaned throughout Coughlin's book.

Chapter 10 The Godfather

1. James Lee Burke, *The Tin Roof Blowdown* (New York: Simon & Schuster, 2007), 76.

2. Karoki, "Happy Fathers Day to all Dads," The Strange Paradox of Events in the Life of an African Son, http://josephkaroki.blogspot.com/2005/06/happy-fathers-day-to-all-dads.html.

3. Ernest Hemingway, "The Capital of the World," in *The Short Stories* (New York: Scribner, 1997), 43.

4. R. Scott Rappold, "Sins of the Father Destine Sons for Prison," *Gazette* (Colorado Springs), October 29, 2006, http://findarticles.com/p/articles/mi_qn4191/is_20061029/ai_n16823829.

5. Antwone Fisher, *Antwone Fisher*, directed by Denzel Washington (Fox Searchlight Pictures, 2002).

Chapter 11 The Adventures of Indiana Jones

1. Johnson, *Man Whisperer*, 36.

Rick Johnson is the founder of Better Dads, a fathering skills program designed to equip men to be more engaged in the lives of their children. He develops and delivers inspirational workshops across the country for businesses, churches, civic groups, social service agencies, hospitals, prisons, and schools. At the request of local school districts, Rick also developed a seminar for single mothers entitled "Courageous Moms: Raising Boys to Become Good Men." He is also the author of *The Man Whisperer*; *Better Dads, Stronger Sons*; and *That's My Son*. Rick and his wife, Suzanne, have two (almost) adult children and live in Gresham, Oregon.

To find out more about Rick Johnson, his books, and the Better Dads/Courageous Moms ministry, or to schedule workshops, seminars, or speaking engagements, please visit www.betterdads.net.

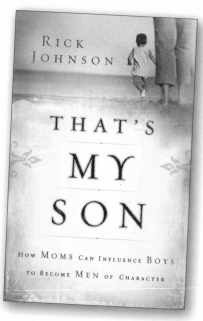
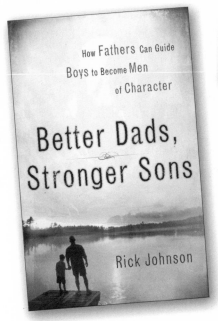
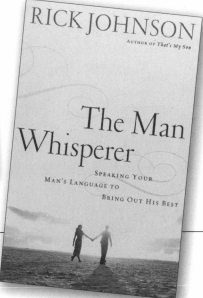